Enjoy!

[signature]

Aria
song of a life

RIKI TUROFSKY

iUniverse

ARIA- SONG OF A LIFE

Copyright © 2014 Riki Turofsky.

All rights reserved. No part of this book may be used or reproduced by any means, graphic, electronic, or mechanical, including photocopying, recording, taping or by any information storage retrieval system without the written permission of the publisher except in the case of brief quotations embodied in critical articles and reviews.

iUniverse books may be ordered through booksellers or by contacting:

iUniverse
1663 Liberty Drive
Bloomington, IN 47403
www.iuniverse.com
1-800-Authors (1-800-288-4677)

Because of the dynamic nature of the Internet, any web addresses or links contained in this book may have changed since publication and may no longer be valid. The views expressed in this work are solely those of the author and do not necessarily reflect the views of the publisher, and the publisher hereby disclaims any responsibility for them.

Any people depicted in stock imagery provided by Thinkstock are models, and such images are being used for illustrative purposes only.
Certain stock imagery © Thinkstock.

ISBN: 978-1-4917-4395-9 (sc)
ISBN: 978-1-4917-4396-6 (hc)
ISBN: 978-1-4917-4397-3 (e)

Library of Congress Control Number: 2014914108

Printed in the United States of America.

iUniverse rev. date: 08/13/2014

Dedication
For Charles, my soulmate and great love of my life, and Carrie, my ever-shining star.

Acknowledgment:
I thank my sister and best friend, Carol Slatt, herself a survivor of many challenges in life, for being there for me at all times, then and now. I love that she is always ready to laugh at my stories and, amazingly, never asked to read any of this book as I was writing it. She will wonder why I got all the facts wrong about our life together. It is, of course, my truth.

That also goes for anyone else whom I have mentioned in this book: It is from my vantage point, and I apologize if the memory of my experiences doesn't match yours.

I thank my sister-in-law, Jane Burfield, a writer herself, who very generously supported me in this endeavour, and Julie Gibson who from the very beginning encouraged me to write my story.

I am grateful to Wayson Choy, whom I met at Humber College's Summer Writing School. He made me believe that I could write my story and not only gave me encouragement, direction, and constructive criticism, but also convinced me to delve deep into my emotions that had been hidden for so long.

Thank you to Susan Valentine, who read the beginning efforts, helped guide me, and gave me the confidence that I had a compelling story to tell, and to Michael Levine for his belief in me.

Thanks to Sylvia Fraser, a brilliant writer who took on the task of editing this book. It has been a journey with Sylvia that I have relished and enjoyed. I am impressed with her attention to detail, memory of facts, and conviction that my story should be told.

Foreword:
"Time present and time past/Are both perhaps present in time future," wrote T.S. Eliot in The Four Quartets and I found myself thinking of his words as I read Aria, by my dear friend, Riki Turofsky.

She calls her memoir "Song of a Life" and that is indeed what it is, a song filled with the melodic richness of love, the harsh dissonance of unkind fates and the healing resolution of someone who has reached that glorious place in life where the singer and the song are truly one.

I first encountered Riki in Vancouver, 40 years ago, at a New Year's Eve Viennese Celebration we were involved in for the Vancouver Symphony Orchestra. She was the dazzling singer being hailed as "Canada's sexy soprano," and I was the up and coming young director christened "the Noel Coward of the Pepsi Generation."

Of course, we had to meet.

We were very different people then and we're still very different people now. She's classy, I'm brassy. She's Schubert and I'm Sondheim. But we both cherish honesty, friendship and someone who is devoted to their art. That's what we found in each other and has held us together over the sometimes stormy decades.

I once heard it said that the entire vista of a relationship is revealed to you in its very first day. That happened with me and Riki.

On one of those incredibly pressured days during which classical concerts come together, we forged a common artistic language. I helped her achieve a needed stillness in one of her solos, she assisted me in helping to tame her high-spirited co-star for the evening and we exchanged a genuinely friendly embrace before the curtain rose.

But watching from the back of the Queen Elizabeth Theatre, I also had the opportunity to see Riki's art in full flower. The aria was Strauss's "Vilia" from *The Merry Widow*, a moment of pure, heartbreaking romantic yearning in the midst of all the operetta high-jinx. A reminder that the leading character is, indeed, a widow and has loved and lost. I can still see Riki, bathed in magenta light, floating slowly across the stage, trying to reconnect with her dreams one more time. Her trademark blonde hair was in those appropriate sausage curls, her dress was layers of shimmering white and her voice was an Alpine mountain stream: clear, cool, refreshing.

Time can play tricks with memory, but I'm pretty sure that she was singing Lorenz Hart's English translation of the lyrics, which give an added poignancy to the moment. Although her youth had known its share of troubles, Riki was standing now at the threshold of her great career, but all of the personal tragedies that were also to lie ahead couldn't have been known to any of us at the moment. And yet she sang with a prescience that was past comprehension.

"Vilia, oh Vilia, I've waited so long/Lonely with only a song." And she looked out at the audience with a mixture of hope and fear that was chilling.

That moment has stayed in my memory for forty years. She's not lonely any more and the song has proven to be her life. Not *only* a song, this one has proved meaningful to all of her friends.

With Aria, she opens that circle of friends to include the world. You will recognize the melody. It's truly universal.

Richard Ouzounian
Toronto, Ontario Aug. 5, 2014

Contents

Overture—Preface xi
Quartetto—My Family 1944–1952 1
Scherzo—Happy Days 1952–1959 15
Movement Triste—Sad Times 1959–1961 23
Chaconne—Many Changes 1961–1965 32
Divertimento—New Adventures 1965–1967 48
A Capella—The Singer 1967–1968 63
Da Capo—Back to the Beginning and Onward 1968–1970 85
Accelerando— Moving along Rapidly 1970–1972 98
Minuet and Trio—The Family Gels 1972–1974 112
Allegretto—Time Passing Quickly 1974–1981 120
Rubato—Changes 1981–1984 129
Lamento—Sorrowful Time 1985 147
Continuo—Life Goes On 1985–1987 155
Postlude —And Beyond June 2012–2014 176
Appendix—Career Highlights 183
About the Author 191

Overture—Preface

I have often been asked, "How did you become an opera singer?"

Typically, I would respond with a much-repeated story of hearing the Canadian Opera Company perform when I was living in Whitehorse; divorcing a cheating husband; moving as a single mother with my one-year-old daughter to Vancouver; learning some arias by listening to a recording, nailing an audition, and *voila!* an opera singer was born. The reaction to this thumbnail review of my life was always "Have you thought about writing a book?"

Intrigued by that idea, I spent years wrestling with *Memoir of an Opera Singer*. I was sure readers would be riveted by my thrilling international performances in front of thousands, my brushes with prime ministers, royalty, and movie stars, along with my exhilaration at soaring over the orchestra with my high notes at Lincoln Center. Oh, the glamour of it all!

After reading a draft of my memoir, friends gently informed me that I had it all wrong. While it's true that I'd been a household name in classical music circles, sung anthems at ball games, hosted TV shows, and appeared on the cover of *Maclean's* magazine, that was decades ago. Now, I was more used to such queries as "Do I know you? You look familiar. I recognize your name. You're someone famous, aren't you?"

What piqued the interest of my early readers were the sketches of my childhood, overshadowed by the unexpected deaths of both of my parents, one from suicide; my two marriages ending in divorce; and every parent's greatest dread, the tragic death of my only child, followed by the discovery of my soulmate.

They felt that I had been skipping over my life's tough parts and hiding my pain in the wonderful parts. In their view, I was a survivor who had faced down the darkest of challenges to create a positive future. They felt that I had an inspiring story to share with others, and they wanted that story in depth.

Strangely, I had never considered myself a survivor, just a person who had managed to work through some bad luck to find good luck. I was an optimist with a naturally sunny disposition; or was that just what I had trained myself to be and to believe?

Spurred on by these comments, I tackled the task of telling my whole story—the tragedies as well as the triumphs—a secure and happy childhood cut short by two deaths, my journey into womanhood, the evolution of my singing talent, love, betrayal, more love, another death, and finally the coming to terms with it all.

Once started, I became so immersed in the clamour of memories that I couldn't stop. I had been warned that the deeper I dug into my feelings, the more my tears would flow. And they did.

"Whoever survives a test, whatever it may be, must tell the story. That is his duty." Elie Wiesel

Aria: In opera, a musical work for solo voice that expresses the innermost thoughts and feelings of an operatic character. Arias provide moments of reflection for the character as well as opportunities for lyrical expression in the opera.

Quartetto—My Family 1944–1952

I remember a childhood overflowing with happiness and security, fun-filled family car trips, scrumptious food, and much music. I also remember when all that came to an abrupt and tragic end.

"Isn't she adorable and clever!" our neighbours exclaimed when I stood on their front porches and sang *I'm a Little Teacup* and asked to be paid. I was three at the time. I loved the praise and the money. That certainly continued as I grew up to become an opera singer.

We lived in Toronto's Forest Hill, the Upper Village, which wasn't as classy as the Lower Village, but was a lot better than downtown near Kensington, where many other Jewish families lived.

My mother, Ruth, was a change-of-life baby. That meant nothing to me when I first heard that as a child, but it explained why her siblings were twenty years older. She had been a sad and lonely little girl, who sat on a stoop outside her family home on Montrose Avenue in Toronto. I learned that she had been born on Queen Street near the mental hospital, known then as an insane asylum. I tried to find some connection between that location and her depression that came when I was a teen, but it was a stretch.

She learned to play the piano by ear and could play almost everything. She once told me that her music kept her from being melancholy. When she played our piano, a Mason & Rich baby grand, my mother was in her element. It was always up-tempo lively music that held me enthralled. I sang all the time, and Mommy accompanied me, while Daddy listened to our rousing melodies. Music was my special bond with my mother. The other was food.

Ruth Rosalind Siegel married at twenty-nine, late in those days. She chose my father, Lou, who was a photographer mostly of sporting events.

He was sixteen years her senior and an unusual choice, as most Jewish girls at that time married men in the trades like furriers, jewellers, or tailors or, if they were lucky, professional men like doctors, dentists, or accountants.

When she was young, my mother was blond and lithe, distinctly different in her Aryan good looks from the many European Jewish girls in Toronto. My parents married in 1937, only six weeks after the death of my mother's mother. Although she looks quite serene in a long white satin gown holding calla lilies in the formal sepia photos, there is an underlying sorrow in Ruth's eyes. I understand that she wanted to postpone or even cancel the wedding party, but it went on.

After her marriage, my mother gained considerable weight. I was skinny and when we cuddled in bed, my bony body found a nice cushion in her warm rich one. She talked about being stout and tried to diet. My mother was pretty and, no matter what size dress she wore, she could pull off looking splendid when she wanted to.

When she was depressed and sick years later, she lost most of the extra poundage, but I liked her better when she was heavy. I once called her a big fat horse, an expression I had heard on the radio. I thought it comical, but it obviously stung, as she sent me down to the basement as punishment. I learned a lesson then about telling the truth and how it could hurt people. I think carefully before I do that now.

My mother had beautiful pale blue eyes, silky fair hair, and high cheek bones. Her regular permanents each summer put waves in her hair, and she went to the hairdresser every Friday so that she could look her best for the weekend. I think she had manicures, but I am not certain. Her hands were not pretty, being rather thick with large unattractive thumbs. But she had style.

My father, Louis Joseph Turofsky, was born in Chicago but moved to Toronto with his family when he was a teen. My parents met when my mother went to him to get her picture taken, knowing Daddy was a bachelor. The rest is my history.

My father had an oval face with a very high forehead. He had almost black wavy hair, deep blue eyes, and a straight nose. He wasn't tall, about five foot seven, with slim legs, and he needed suspenders to hold up his socks on those legs. Proud of his hands, he had manicures regularly, as he hated the stain that the photo developer chemicals left on his nails. On his beautiful slender pinky, he sported a gold ring with a tiny diamond in its centre. There was always a cigar in the side of his mouth: He hardly ever smoked it, but he sucked on it a great deal, and it became his trademark. Old Spice was his chosen aftershave. Enchanted with the scent, I fell in love with a boy at a dance, just because he was soaked in it; well, fell in love for the length of one song.

I adored Daddy and he me. I would lie against his stomach, which was substantial, and he would tickle my back. We would often listen to the Metropolitan Opera broadcasts together. He loved his Texaco Saturdays, somehow teaching me about music while I lay there enjoying the sensual touch of his fingers. Once I put on a kimono, placed knitting needles in my hair, and pretended I was Madame Butterfly, with an operatic soprano voice that I found somewhere. I pranced into my parents' bedroom and sang my heart out in some made-up language. Their delight was palpable.

Daddy arranged for us all to see the Metropolitan Opera Company on tour at Toronto's Maple Leaf Gardens, a hockey arena transformed. It was a performance of *Rigoletto* with Roberta Peters, Robert Merrill, and Richard Tucker, a dream cast in an opera that I was to perform years later and one that would be the first for me to learn as a fledgling singer: My father would have been overjoyed to hear me sing Gilda.

Everyone knew and liked my father. Much of his working time was spent at the track, where he covered the horse races for the newspapers. He pioneered a Canadian version of the photo-finish camera, which precisely captured the horses speeding across the finish line. We were shown a *Liberty* magazine article about this, with pictures of him demonstrating how it worked, and how it was immediately used to determine the result of two close finishes at its debut in 1937. But he wasn't a businessman and lost the Canadian patent on this brilliant idea, which was the basis for the sensor called the electric eye, a device that automatically opens doors. We might have been millionaires, but we weren't. Not even close.

Daddy hung out with his younger brother Nat at their shared office downtown in the old *Toronto Star* building on King Street, where their colourful friends from the sports world would often join them. The office had a not-unpleasant odour of men, tobacco, and photofinisher. The walls were covered with massive black and white photographs of hockey players and horses, mounted on boards. But the *Miss Toronto* ones, with swimsuit contestants wearing banners across their chests and their long tanned bare legs ending in high-heeled pumps, absorbed me.

Daddy was known for sports, but he had an artistic soft side. There was a shot of a gawky young tattered newspaper boy asleep on a street curb, and another of a very old woman with hairy eyebrows and weathered skin, smoking a pipe. Those were magical. On the walls were photos of the Queen Mother, Roosevelt with Mackenzie King, and the Duke of Windsor beside his American divorcée; I loved the sound of that last word.

On the walls were a few shiny pictures of my father and uncle Nat with their cronies. I liked the ones that showed Daddy on an iceboat or, as a kid, in an old-fashioned baseball uniform or football gear. He was an outdoorsman and an athlete. I came honestly by my love of sports.

Next to the office was a cigar store that sold candies. At Christmastime, Daddy bought me Lifesavers in a silver box that looked like a thick book, which I could open and see the individual packages of all the flavours laid out in rows like sentences. My favourite was butter rum. Daddy knew I loved *reading* those books.

I wasn't fond of the bathroom in his office: It was dingy, with tiny cracked bits of soap and a shared towel. On one visit, I made a disapproving remark about the janitor who was cleaning it. Daddy stopped me right then and there. "Don't you ever think you are better than anyone else, young lady, just because you were born into a good home and have everything you want. You must always treat everyone the same whether they are royalty or a ditch digger." I never forgot that lesson.

My father made no effort to hide how much he loved me. I was his baby. Every night when I went to bed, he came to my room and kissed me. He would make this loud noise like *boodger* and blow on my neck until I giggled and quieted down. After he left, I would sing out, "I wanna drinka wataaa!" He would bring me a cup of water from the bathroom and say goodnight again. Daddy always came when I called, even though he knew I wasn't a bit thirsty. He made me feel safe. He smelled good. He was mine forever, or so I thought.

My sister, Carol Sue Turofsky, was three years and nine months older than me. She always stressed the exact age difference rather than rounding it up to four; she still does. She was blond, blue-eyed, and angelic-looking as a young child. She had fair skin and large white teeth, which we called buck teeth. As a teen, she never seemed to have an ugly or awkward stage. When she was thirteen, she looked like Grace Kelly, and was already very developed. As she grew older, she wore her hair in a French roll. Everyone said she was the beautiful one and I was the talented one. For some reason, that didn't bother me. My parents told us all the time that they loved us equally when we asked, "Which one of us do you love the best?"

Carol was voluptuous and wore clothes confidently with great panache. She had more dates than she knew what to do with, but she always ran late getting ready, so I spent time with the guys, chatting them up. I guess it was worth the wait, as they kept coming back. When we were young, our mother delighted in dressing us in identical outfits; unfortunately, I later inherited the same clothes from my sister. Carol and my mother were very close and enjoyed shopping together, while I traipsed after my father, delivering pictures to the newsrooms or going to a baseball game.

As the older sister, Carol bossed me around. She always assumed she was right about everything, and she often was; but as I grew up, I formed opinions of my own and started to assert myself. Nevertheless, I mostly deferred to her. That really hasn't changed much now that we are older and are best friends who share our deepest thoughts. We talk or text almost every day no matter where we are in the world. Best of all, we share the same humour, amusing-only-to-us sort of situations, that bring on gales of uninhibited laughter.

Carol was my idol. Dating from an early age, she always seemed so mature, wearing lipstick and a bra when she was twelve, the blue-eyed blond the boys loved. On the other hand, I had dirty blond hair and thick dark eyebrows that she plucked to almost nothing when I was thirteen. At that time, I started putting lemon juice in my hair so that it streaked blonder in the sun. She was well-built, and I was skinny. She had the best bedroom, and it seemed she had her way all the time, unless I was clever enough to get her into trouble with our parents. And I was.

My room was near my sister's. I liked mine because it had a pink wooden scallop around the ceiling and a ledge where all my dolls could be displayed. But I coveted my sister's enormous room. I knew that someday she would get married and it would be mine. I could barely wait. She even had a double bed with matching furniture that had a creamy glossy veneer.

I loved my home. Even now, it is our place at 113 Wembley Road that features in my dreams. Our kitchen was large enough to have a table and later a Bendix Duomatic washer/dryer combination that I marvelled at. We didn't have a television then, so watching the clothes go around through the glass window in the door was mesmerizing.

We ate most of our meals in a separate yellow breakfast room. A canary once had his cage there and sang along with the radio. *Teddy Bears' Picnic* was his favourite. I don't remember him, but I often heard that song on CBC radio. It started out rather scarily in a minor key, "If you go down in the woods today, you're in for a big surprise...." Then, there they were, all the teddy bears sitting around having a picnic and enjoying themselves, and it ended cheerily in a major key.

I really wanted a pet of my own. "There will be no more pets in this house," my mother said tearily. I wondered why she couldn't just replace that little bird with a dog or something, but years later I understood how she felt when I lost my first beloved pet, Clara the cat. Mommy was so attached to a bird; how would she react if some person she loved died?

We had wall-to-wall carpet everywhere in the house, except in the big bathroom, where there were tiny white and black tiles on the floor and on the walls. Our mailbox was actually a milkbox by the side door. I loved getting letters. Every morning we would hear a tenor voice sing "Mailman" and know that the day's news had arrived. For years, I dreamt about that milkbox bursting with letters all addressed to me.

Below the landing, more stairs led to the basement. The walls had some sort of ridged woody veneer, and there was a bar that we never used. The smell was not musty exactly downstairs, but cool and unfriendly. A cedar cupboard, housing most of our winter clothes, exuded an aroma that I savoured when I opened the heavy double doors. A creepy furnace room with an uneven cement floor contained an old locked trunk; I always wondered what was in it but never found out. The cold room stored bottles of ginger ale and canned goods. Hating to be sent there at night to fetch things, I would go down carefully step by step and grab what I needed, and then race up the stairs, certain that some creature was following close behind. I still don't like going down to my basement at night, although I am now a very big girl. I convince myself that there are no more bogeymen, but I never linger.

We had two bathrooms, one for all of us that had a large tub and shower combination, and a smaller one with just a sink and toilet, near the maid's room. We didn't have a maid, but I had heard that, many years before, Orma lived with us and helped out. She came from Manitoulin Island, wherever that was, and I saw a picture of her. She had a big mole on her face with a long disgusting black hair attached. I wondered why she just didn't take a scissors and cut it off. I used to play under the brass bed in her room. My friends would join me, and we would amuse ourselves with my dolls and our imaginations. It was our secret place.

My mother was a terrific cook and hostess. When I came home from school for lunch, the smells from the kitchen would waft through to the front door. Mommy made the best *kreplach* in the world. She prepared them with meat from leftover roast that she ground by hand with a steel meat grinder attached to an ironing board, which magically came out of the kitchen wall. I loved to see the squiggly bits of meat falling into the bowl and getting stuffed into little packets of dough, before they were dropped into hot chicken soup. As I write this, I can almost taste them. I would gaze with hunger and desire and beg, "Mommy, let me try some to see if they are any good." She always let me sample them because I was thin: I think she made extra for just that reason. If I am sick now, all I want are *kreplach* and chicken soup. My sister usually gets me some in the Jewish neighbourhood where she lives today. They are not like my mother's, but they satisfy me in a very primitive way.

My mother made all kinds of delicacies—thick vegetable soups filled with soft carrots brewed in a deep kettle on the stove; savory ground veal, rice, and tomatoes in silky cabbage rolls; cheese *blintzes* with just the right amount of cinnamon served with chilled sour cream on Thursday nights when we didn't eat meat; meatballs with simple boiled potatoes and French's mustard on the side; the best crispy southern fried chicken with honey; meat pies made with home-ground steak topped with mashed potatoes and then baked in the oven in a pie dish until a crust formed, which I make today with lamb and call shepherd's pie. I salivate as I remember those meals. Her baking was outstanding, too. We would wake to the intoxicating smell of yeast rising to become *puder kuchen/* cinnamon buns, or sometimes she'd surprise us with luscious apple pies filled with vanilla and brown sugar.

Friday nights for Sabbath dinner, Mommy fixed something very special, like broiled chicken with pineapple slices on top and a maraschino cherry in the middle, and we ate at the dining-room table set with all her finest china and silverware. Covering her eyes with her hands, she would say a prayer over the candles; then Daddy would say one over the sickly sweet Manischewitz wine that we had to drink; and finally we said one over the soft fresh chewy *challah* from Louis's bakery. After the prayer rituals, we would eat.

We learned good manners at those meals of many courses. Embossed linen napkins rested on our laps, and we were told which utensil to use for which food. "Don't slurp your chicken soup, Rickey. Sip it elegantly and silently, and move your spoon *away* from the edge of the soup bowl." I certainly never forgot what I learned at that table, nor did my sister, who still carries on the Friday night dinner tradition in her home.

Most Sunday nights, we went out for dinner, with my sister and I dressed up with white gloves and patent Mary Jane shoes. At the Royal York Hotel, I chose roast beef and mashed potatoes; and at Chez Paris, chicken à la king called "Pinocchio" on the children's menu. We became very comfortable in elegant restaurants at an early age. Even then, we knew which were the best tables. My mother told us, "Never ever be seated by the kitchen door." Today when I go out to eat with my husband, I am allowed to pick my table once, no changing. I am fussy about where I sit, and so is my sister. Thanks, Mommy.

My mother was very proud of her belongings, particularly her beautiful home. She was content with being a homemaker and took pride in all that entailed. She did volunteer work at the hospital, played mah-jong with her girlfriends, or went to Buffalo on shopping excursions. Occasionally, she used her pianist skills and accompanied the synagogue choir. She seemed happy enough, although I am sure she would have liked to be richer and more financially secure. My father's money from his photography came in lumps, when he did a special job for the racetrack. His regular pay came from the newspapers.

Although my mother's friends were richer, *she* had exquisite taste. Over the chesterfield hung a large oil painting of an English pastoral scene called *Gossips by the Roadside*, which my parents bought because the model for both of the poses looked like my beautiful sister. We were told it was very valuable. I loved looking at it and wished I had been allowed to rub my fingers over the bumps the oil made.

Our backyard was filled with sweet perfumed lilac trees and aromatic peonies. I played in the street. I loved skipping rope, mostly double Dutch, and creating plays with the other kids, and watching anything on a neighbour's new television, the first on the block. At the corner lived a real gangster who had a gun. Across the street lived a boy with cerebral palsy. There was a politician who threw garden parties. There were Jews and Gentiles. It was a miniature world.

We regularly held the family *shivas*—the ritual during the week of mourning after a Jewish funeral—at our house. People visited either during the day or in the evening to pay their respects and bring chocolates. I cherished those, particularly Black Magic, because I knew which pieces were which and didn't have to squeeze every chocolate until I found a nice hard one: nobody liked it when I did that. Even going to the funerals in limos wasn't bad, because most of the dead didn't mean anything to me. They were just old aunts, cousins, and a hunchbacked grandfather from Russia whom I hardly knew—remembering only his scratchy beard and sour breath when he kissed me in the nursing home where he lived. Little did I know how important *shivas* would be in my life, more than the chocolates for sure.

Sunday afternoons, we had musical gatherings at our house for the relatives. In the family circle, Mommy, Carol, and I were known as the Three Alley Cats. I just started harmonizing naturally in tunes like "Down by the Riverside" and "Heart of My Heart". My real talent though was belting out Kay Starr and Teresa Brewer hits like "Music Music Music" and raunchy numbers of Sophie Tucker that I didn't understand but made everyone chuckle. I loved making people laugh; I still do. Carol could carry a tune and liked singing but really was in my shadow in the music-making department. I just loved those afternoons when we all made music together. It seemed so natural. I thought every family did that.

We weren't the only performers either. Cousin Nina and her son Barry were extremely musical. My mother was her aunt, even though she was younger. Nina, who must have been in her early forties, was the same size as I was at eight years of age. My mother explained, "My sister is much older than I am, so her daughter is, too." It didn't make any sense to me. My mother was closer to her niece than to her own sister Sadie, who was a small sad shrivelled sort of woman. She never smiled, not that I can remember.

In the sitting room of Sadie's house was a Victrola that played "The Bluebird of Happiness", a wimpy sort of tune that stuck in my head. "Be like I, hold your head up high, you will find the bluebird of happiness..." and it went on in a very "look on the bright side of things sort of spirit", a sentiment that made a strong impression and influenced how I dealt with what life later threw at me.

Other relatives appeared from time to time at our musical afternoons, like Uncle Jonas, Mommy's older brother, who had sparse grey hair and a stubbly chin and wore colourless glasses. Aunt Ada, his wife, had a pinched face with olive skin and dark rings in soft flaps under her eyes. I didn't like my aunt and uncle much, even though Aunt Ada made the best lemon meringue pie ever. I was prescient in not liking them, as I found out later on when things turned bad and I had to live with them. They had two sons who were okay, even though they were boys.

Sometimes Cousin Elliot and his crazy wife, Pearl, visited. A highly respected dentist in Toronto, Elliot was the son of Mommy's brother. Pearl was in and out of mental institutions, but supposedly was brilliant. Again, a cousin was closer in age to Mommy than her brother, more confusion for my little mind. Cousin Elliot had an Ampex tape recorder and captured the Three Alley Cats singing. Much hilarity followed when we heard ourselves for the first time.

My parents' twin beds were pushed together to look like one big one, the way some hotels do now, except they didn't have a large king bedspread. When I was sick, they let me sleep in their room, and Mommy would wipe my fever down with a cool washcloth, bring me chocolate puddings with a skin on top and Lipton's chicken noodle soup. I would lay there happily, all cuddled up, listening to recordings of *South Pacific* and *The King and I*, that were all the rage. I learned the lyrics of every song and could copy the performers perfectly. I would dream I was on stage singing the best Nellie Furbush anyone had ever heard. I was sure that my life was a movie, and I was the star performer.

I detested synagogue, sitting for hours in my scratchy grey wool suit. My skin was oily, and the feel of the wool against it was dreadful. I hated the stale smell of the men's breath that hovered in the air on a Saturday morning. I couldn't read Hebrew, so I just learned the singsongy bits by rote. I really should have been in some church choir singing like an angel with my high soprano instead of sitting mimicking the men's chants in the *shul*.

Although I didn't like the formality of religion, I did say my prayers faithfully every night. I had a long list of people I prayed for. This list would change from time to time, and I still can't fall asleep unless I go through this ritual. I am not sure that God was ever listening, but it consoled me in some strange way, and still does.

Aria- song of a life

There was much family harmony, but also a fair amount of discord in our home on Wembley Road. My mother and sister fought often, and my father would join in the fray. I can't remember what the fights were about. I think that when my sister became a teenager, there were some heated discussions about her and her boyfriends and her boyfriends' families, but I don't really remember. Sometimes it was just Mommy and Daddy going at it. Again, I was not party to the details.

I remember Mommy once storming out of the house, slamming the door, getting in her car, and not returning for hours. I had no idea what all the screaming was about, but I ran around and closed the windows, struggling with the venetian blinds, so none of the neighbours could hear. I am not sure that the details of the arguments matter in my story. What *matters* is that tempers would flare and then all would be quiet. It was fast and furious, then over. Finished, done, like a balloon filling up and bursting. No one held a grudge. Things would be normal again, and the laughter would resume. There was always laughter and humour in my house, at least when I was a child.

Our family shared a similar sense of humour, and we would laugh at all sorts of things. As an example, my father was not handy at all around the house, but he loved to fix the plumbing. He would come home from his office, dressed in his suit with tie and long-sleeved shirt with cufflinks, and attack a leaky sink or toilet. Watching him all dressed up and struggling and swearing at the tap, and knowing that Mommy would have to call a plumber in the morning, struck our funny bones. Perhaps we didn't laugh in *front* of him. He wouldn't have been amused. I loved laughing and giggling in school and often was asked to leave the class. For me, it is always situational comedy. Put me in front of a comedian, and I am usually quite stern. I just don't get slapstick either.

I think that my parents had a good marriage. They were very affectionate with each other. They slept together, well, close enough in their two twin beds pushed together. They laughed, travelled (mostly with us), entertained, had friends over for regular evenings, and saw their relatives. They made my sister and me feel very secure and happy in our lives. We had dinner together as a family most nights of the week. I think my mother was proud to have a husband who was a celebrity. People were always asking about whether we were related to the famous photographer, when they heard our name, which we often spelled out carefully—T as in Tom, U R O F as in Frank, S as in Sam, K Y.

My mother was delighted with my father's achievements. She depended on him, loved him, and catered to him. That was her role as a housewife, but I think she was a half-empty cup kind of person, rather than a half-full type. As a child of this marriage and the younger one, I can only guess. But I was joyful and content all the time in my cozy nest.

As a family, we travelled a great deal. After a special photography job, my father would get a very big fee and buy a new car. I remember a Buick with large portholes on the fenders and the excitement that ran through me. We would pack up swiftly and set off for Cape Cod in the summers, to resorts like Buttermilk Bay Inn on Buzzards Bay, places where there were white rockers on large airy porches and where the smell of the sea floated on the breeze. In the winters, when we were still young, my parents would take us out of school for a month and we would head down to Florida for the baseball spring-training camps, where my father worked covering the Maple Leaf baseball team for the Toronto papers. He would announce, "We're off to Florida. Pack your bags!"

All the way south, I would stand in the back of the car and sing in my father's right ear. I went from song to song, driving everyone crazy. It was a long way to Florida, so when I tired of singing and games, we would turn on the radio. Mostly the reception wasn't good, but we liked *The Jack Benny Show* with Rochester and Dennis Day. I would start singing again really loudly if *Abbott and Costello* came on: I hated that show. Once we settled in Miami I performed daily for all the guests at the apartment complex. "I've Got a Lovely Bunch of Coconuts" was my Florida song.

I was so excited about the family trips, I could hardly sleep the night before we left. I would be up at 5:00 in the morning and run around waking everyone else. As we'd put the bags in the trunk the night before, we were ready to roll on our adventure at dawn. My father was a very slow driver, unlike my mother, the eighty-miles-an-hour-plus speeder. We kidded him mercilessly about passing the same tree for ten minutes. "Daddy, we're watching this tree grow!" we would shout from the back seat.

I would check out all the bathrooms in the gas stations and restaurants. I have no idea why. Perhaps it was for a change of scene or some guidebook I was planning to write about the best and worst washrooms on the highway to Florida. *Trip Advisor* would have loved me. One time, I insisted on getting the bathroom key from the gas station attendant and visiting the facilities, even though I had just been in a restaurant and really didn't have to go. When I came back to the pumps, I looked around and couldn't see our car anywhere. I stood there frozen and then started to cry. Moments later, the car rounded the station with all their smiling faces plastered to the windows. Even though it was only for a brief time, I felt what it was like to be abandoned.

Little did I know that sad lonely sense of loss would return with a vengeance.

My parents wedding portrait 1937

Riki Turofsky

Sisters, Carol and Riki at 7 and 3 years 1947

Family on Vacation in Atlantic City circa 1949

Scherzo—Happy Days 1952–1959

My early school years were spent at West Prep Elementary, about five blocks north of where we lived. I walked every day and picked up a girlfriend on the way. She was the prettiest girl in the class, petite and perfect with naturally curly hair—and I had to have a smelly cold-wave permanent every summer. Once I was caught in the rain after school and ended up looking like Kurly Kate and stinking of ammonia. Suzie was always dressed flawlessly; with neat little ankle socks trimmed in lace and pleated plaid skirts with matching sweaters and blouses. Not only did she look adorable, she was good at everything. Her house was *Good Housekeeping* perfectly kept, but it never smelled as good as ours. Her mother, who was young, beautiful, and slim, always teased me lovingly about my boy's name. She called me Ricky Ricardo, like Lucy's husband. I was infatuated with her.

I loved school and sat at the front of the class. There was only one teacher, Miss Olive Robb, who wouldn't call me Rickey. "You must have a girl's name!" she hissed. So she called me Rita, the name I was given at birth, a name that was never used except by that narrow-minded woman and on my passport in later years. She was the one who made us repeat the times tables as fast as we could. I hated arithmetic from that day on and still struggle with it, but have no trouble reciting from memory the numbers on my credit card.

I took music in grade seven, studying theory, singing, and ear training for pitch control. I disliked the theory, probably because it was another form of mathematics. I already knew my aptitude for that, but the singing and ear training were a breeze. Mr. Bradshaw, the music teacher, took me aside and pronounced, "Rickey, you'll have to study the violin if you want to take music in junior high."

Because of the theory, he had just failed me, even though I was a natural musician with more talent than all the other kids put together and certainly more ego. My punishment was to be in the strings class. Obviously, they were desperate for string players, everyone wanting to play trumpet or clarinet. But I didn't care if I had no choice of instrument. I would still be in the music class, and with a vengeance.

That year, I realized I had been bypassed in the bust department. All the girls were developed, but me. I was flat as a boy, and prayed fervently every night, *Dear God, please give me breasts.* None were forthcoming. I was doomed to be boyish forever, like my name.

Despite the lack of a bust, I had a really good male best friend, Michael Benjamin. His father was an undertaker, with a monopoly on Jewish funerals. When the kids teased him, Michael always said he would never go into that business. Many years later, he did exactly that. Ironically, he became a comfort to me in his chosen profession.

We had a terrific time together, and I was invited to marvellous parties at his house. One was a Halloween dress-up, to which I went as Doris Day in *Lullaby of Broadway*. My father rented a top hat and small tails from Malabar's costume house, where I was to spend a lot of time in later years. I wore black silk shorts, sheer net stockings, and patent pumps. When I wanted, I could sing just like Doris. Some of the kids had even heard me when I was eight years old at junior camp, where I stood on a chair and sang Doris Day's pop songs to much acclaim.

Forest Hill Collegiate held Halloween parties every year. Once, I went as a gypsy with cards sewn to my skirt. Another year, I went as a fat Aunt Jemima stuffed with pillows into one of my mother's housedresses. I was slathered in Hershey's chocolate syrup to make me dark and wore a bandana on my head. Hard to imagine a kid wearing black face in today's world, but in 1954 when I was ten, there really weren't any black folks in Toronto, certainly not in my world.

We knew of Aunt Jemima from the pancake mix box. Both my sister and mother thought it would be perfect for me. So did I. On the way out of the auditorium, I slipped and fell, and it seemed liked hundreds of screaming kids walked over me. It was horrifying. I couldn't breathe, and even now, when I think about being trapped, I start to panic and hyperventilate. If I find myself in an enclosed space, it's worse still.

When my sister and I arrived home, I had to be thrown into the bathtub to soften and remove the dried syrup mixed with tears on my skin. I could feel every hair on my arms, as my mother and sister yanked the goo from them. They didn't stop laughing the whole time. I was so angry at them for making fun of me, but all I could do was cry. I am still a crier when it comes to arguments, which really ruins the point I want to make. It is rare that I get into fights now.

Michael and I were together when I first heard Bill Haley's "Rock Around the Clock". (Our parents insisted that rock and roll wouldn't last!) Michael took me to some great parties. At one in Hamilton, we danced to "Blue Suede Shoes" by a sexy-sounding singer, who Michael told me was Elvis Presley. I was enraptured, and I wasn't the only one. Elvis was coming to Toronto to play at Maple Leaf Gardens. Since my father knew everyone there, I begged, "Daddy, please, if you love me, get me tickets please. Daddy, please."

He sent me with Mrs. Watson, his secretary's mother, who was about a hundred years old, but I didn't care. We went on the new Toronto subway, and sat in a box close to the stage. In his one-piece skin-tight jumpsuit, Elvis writhed and wiggled. I screamed and screamed. So did Mrs. Watson and everyone else. I had never experienced anything like that. My sexuality was awakened, but I didn't quite know what it was or how to handle it. I felt shivery all over when I thought of Elvis. When he appeared on the the *Ed Sullivan Show*, I screamed some more. My parents just smiled and watched with my sister and me.

Ed Sullivan was a weekly ritual, as was *Jackie Gleason* on Saturday nights, *American Bandstand*, and *The Mickey Mouse Show*. We watched our new television in our upstairs den as a family, except when my parents had company over to play gin rummy for the men and mah-jong for the women. They drank Cherry Heering and ginger ale, and their laughter, conversation, and cigarette smoke floated upstairs.

When I went to Forest Hill Junior High, I felt quite grown up, although I hadn't done much in the *up* department. I was one of the shortest girls in my grade: At thirteen years, I was under five feet tall. The one advantage to my smallness was that all the majorettes were small, so when I tried out, I was chosen. I was even given a baton and a cute uniform. Because the other girls shaved their legs, I bought a kit that had a mitt in it that felt like sandpaper. I removed the hair from my legs, too. My mother was furious. "You will be a slave to that all your life. You'll be sorry." I never was sorry, as it turned out, and I wasn't a slave, because I had blond hair and not much of it. I liked the way my legs looked and felt. No hairy European legs and armpits for me!

I auditioned for the school musical, *Toad of Toad Hall,* and because of my small stature won a role as a dancing weasel. I had a furry costume complete with snout. For the first time, I experienced the joy of being on stage performing in front of an audience, albeit as a wordless character.

I began the music course as a violinist, but the new music teacher, Mr. Coles, was looking for a volunteer to play string bass. My parents were relieved to have me trade in the squeaky scales of the violin for the sonorous tones of the bass. I became a member of the orchestra in which we played watered-down versions of the classics.

I met my new best friend, Carol Kirsh, in my class. Amazingly, we are still friends, and she has the honour of having attended all three of my weddings. We participated in everything and asked a lot of questions. I played basketball and volleyball, and found the excitement of competition thrilling. I looked forward to school every day, even though I had to take two buses to get there.

In the summers, I'd progressed from family trips to Camp New Moon. I wasn't wild about the idea of living in a cabin with ten other girls, but I learned that camp could be agreeable. I met my first real boyfriend there. Morton Doran was four years older than me and the camp tripper, which meant he took campers out on canoe trips. Mort and I used to sneak out of camp regularly and go to his parents' cottage right beside the property. We didn't do much there other than hang out and eat ice cream, kiss a bit, and drive fast around Lake of Bays in his motorboat. He was quite brilliant and rather unusual, which was probably why he liked a girl who was four years younger and didn't have a bust.

Mort was an excellent tripper, very detailed and reliable. Everyone knew they could trust Morty, the superb canoeist, but he had nervous tics and mannerisms. Years later, he was diagnosed with Tourette syndrome. I liked him tics and all.

He always had a little black comb in his back pocket to keep his fine light brown straight hair just so. His hair bleached in the sun when he tanned and looked really good. Glasses mostly hid his deep-set eyes, but they were almost indigo blue. A high forehead and very white teeth completed the picture, although he didn't smile much. He couldn't dance, which was disappointing because there were many socials. He was five-foot-seven, and well muscled. I was only five feet tall, so his height was not an issue. I really liked the blond hair on his bronze arms. I hadn't started to develop yet, but I liked those arms.

Summer camp was fun. Aside from participating in all the sports, I sang in the camp shows, which were very sophisticated. The musical director, Paul Hoffert, who later played keyboard in the successful rock group Lighthouse, was very accomplished on the piano. I auditioned and won the role of Laurie in *Oklahoma*. Everyone told me I was very good. I knew it myself. My big numbers like "Out of My Dreams" and "People Will Say We're in Love" flowed from my heart. Years later, when I sang them professionally, they were like old friends.

Since I was a child, I had been singing those songs to the recordings from all the musicals in my home—in the den, my bedroom, the living room, and my head. It was a fantasy come true to perform the lead role in costume with dialogue. I wasn't nervous on the stage, but excited. I revelled in the response from the audience. This was a glimpse of how I would feel when I performed professionally, although I didn't know that then.

The summer flew by, and my romance with Morty continued back in the city. He loved me, and I loved having a boyfriend, especially one who could drive and take me out in his own car. I think I did love him as well, but I definitely liked all the rest. His parents were very rich, and he always had money in his back pocket, along with that little black comb.

The following summer after grade nine and before I entered high school, my parents sent me to a different summer camp from Mort's. I think they were trying to separate us, at least my father was. Nevertheless, Mort would drive a few hours every weekend to visit me.

After my arrival at Camp Winnebago, I started to bleed. At fifteen, I finally had my period! I had not come prepared for that momentous event, and the tuck shop was closed. I didn't know any of the other girls, who had been camping together for years. I was an outsider. Fortunately, my counsellor came to the rescue with a supply of Kotex. There was one bunk available in the cabin, and I was on the top in the corner farthest from the toilet. Great!

I had my period for two long weeks. I thought it would never end and, worst of all, my skin broke out in horrible pimples. I was a mess. I was miserable. I took refuge in the stables, because I could shovel dung and ride and be mostly alone. The horses didn't care what I looked like. Of course, I couldn't avoid mealtimes. At the first Friday night Sabbath meal, I was sitting in my whites, when a camp waiter dropped a tray of tomato juice all over me. Perfect!

The following Saturday, my father arrived to take pictures because he was the official camp photographer. I was happy to see him, but on seeing me he said, "Where did you get those pimples? Get rid of them." I burst into tears. As if I could do anything about my face. It was really mean of Daddy to point out my pimples. I think he thought I was his perfect little girl, and all of a sudden I wasn't—not a little girl anymore and certainly not perfect-looking with smooth skin. I was hurt and determined to find a way to get my oily skin dried out and clear. Little did I know then that my oily skin would last for years and would be a blessing. Lots of pimples young, but few wrinkles now.

The one good thing that happened that summer was that I finally got breasts. At last God responded to my prayers. By about the fourth week of camp, the other girls were starting to come around and be friendly to me, but I was booked for only a month. I had to go home, tearfully, on the camp bus.

In August, after I arrived home from camp, boys other than Mort started calling. I guess they didn't notice the pimples, as I learned how to conceal them, but they noticed the breasts. I amazingly grew five inches in height. I had metamorphosed into a new almost grown-up me.

That fall at Forest Hill Collegiate, I auditioned to be a cheerleader and was chosen as one of the lucky eight. I loved going to the games with our teams, in my royal blue and gold uniform. Soon after that, I read about a tryout for the Toronto Argonauts football team cheerleaders. I put in an application for an audition, practised my star jumps and cartwheels, and flipped my hair. My mother drove me to Casa Loma, where they held the auditions. I was all dolled up with makeup and wore a big smile. I felt nervous but really ready. Just as I was about to go in, my father arrived in a fury, grabbed me, and dragged me outside. "No daughter of mine is going to jump around in front of those men!" he shouted as I cried my eyes out, and he rubbed the makeup off my face.

I knew how he felt about me trying to get on shows like *The Ted Mac Amateur Hour*, but I thought the cheerleading was different. I was so talented, and my mother was encouraging, but he would have none of it. I privately liked the idea that my father was so protective. I was actually proud that he cared so much about me. He was a photographer after all and, along with sports, was on the fringes of show business. He saw how children were exploited for their talent and the parents who pushed them. I was not going to be one of those children. He did not want a Shirley Temple but a young girl with a normal upbringing. I think that this made me love him more, once my anger and embarrassment subsided.

I broke up with Mort, whom I really didn't like anymore. I felt bad when I gave him back his fraternity pin, especially when his upper lip curled down and he looked so sad, but I wanted to go out with other guys. I *was* fifteen. He still kept coming around, and I often saw him in our kitchen in deep conversation with my mother. She promised Mort that I would marry him someday and encouraged him. I guess she figured I'd appreciate him and become his wife, as he was going to be a doctor.

It was now 1959: My favourite musical, *West Side Story*, ended its long run on Broadway, and *The Sound of Music* arrived. Barbie Dolls were introduced to wild success, and Khrushchev visited the United States. But most important in my world, my sister was engaged at nineteen.

Never was there so much excitement in our house. She actually wasn't marrying the boy she had been dating, but another one, a rebound I think. Bernard Slatt was different from all the other guys. He was seven years older than Carol and already a doctor. I understood that his family was not worldly or cultured but very rich. His father was smart and owned the successful Serta mattress company. Bernie was the youngest of four children, and his siblings already had children. It was a large close family. My new brother-in-law was brilliant, arrogant, athletic, and sexy, and looked like Leonard Cohen. He had a slick sense of humour, and he was infatuated with my blond, very gentile-looking sister.

The wedding was at our synagogue. There seemed to be hundreds of people there. My mother and sister had worked out every detail to be original and spectacular. As maid-of-honour, I wore a fuchsia satin dress with matching bow for my hair. My sister wore a blush-pink lace gown, and looked resplendent with her hair in a French roll and pearls around her neck. The food presentation was unique: I remember carvery trolleys laden with roast beef. We danced to Benny Lewis's orchestra. I didn't invite Mort, but a gawky tall pink-cheeked guy called Harold. The best part was that I finally got to move into my sister's large bedroom when she moved out. I was elated.

I continued to participate in a multitude of school activities. I played string bass in the orchestra and most weekends in a dance band called The

Blue Rhythm Boys Plus One. Songs like "Pennsylvania Six Five Thousand" and "In the Mood" were part of our repertoire. Once in a while, to my delight, they would let me sing.

Along with competitive team sports, I did archery, track and field, and student council. I received a school key, was chosen the top female athlete, and won the Ontario Leadership Award, which included going to a special athletic summer camp, all expenses paid. I longed to go to that camp. Sadly, I never got the chance.

Riki age thirteen at Camp New Moon 1958

Movement Triste—Sad Times 1959–1961

Suddenly in the middle of the night, I awoke to the sound of my mother shouting. I didn't know what was going on. I was confused and disoriented and very frightened. "Daddy is having a heart attack! Call your sister!" she screamed.

My sister and her new doctor husband lived close by. I made the call immediately, but it was too late. My father died that chilly Wednesday on October 14, 1959. And so did my childhood.

I had been up all night and into the morning with my mother and sister. Some strangers came to the house. I think they were there to take my father's body away, most likely from Michael Benjamin's father's funeral home. I had only a moment to glimpse Daddy's face before he left. It looked very smooth and serene, and he was unnaturally still. He certainly didn't seem like my vibrant father. I felt like I was in some scary movie.

Somehow, I remembered that my friends would be arriving to pick me up for school. The walk from the house down the driveway— less than twenty yards—to meet them was unbearably long. I had to explain why I wasn't going with them. I was so unsteady; I could hardly utter the unreal words as tears started slipping from my eyes. "My father just died."

I remember little more about that morning except people arriving, my mother weeping uncontrollably, and conversations from which I was excluded. There were many extensive newspaper articles about my father and his career with his famous sports photos; he was, after all, a well-known Toronto celebrity. "Lou Turofsky, the famous photographer died of a massive heart attack."

I was proud that he was so admired, but my Daddy was dead. My neat little life was shattered. I was stunned and heartbroken. The house was full of activity—putting soap on the mirrors, one of the many Jewish rituals dealing with death; finding something proper to wear to the funeral; organizing food; dealing with phone calls; shedding copious tears.

Before long, we were in a limousine on our way to the service at Beth Tzedec synagogue, and then the cemetery. I remember little of the service except all of us crying, particularly when cantor Cooper started *davening* and singing his gut-wrenching sorrowful music. I remember reading the English transliteration of the Mourner's Kaddish: "*Yitgadal v'yit-kadash sh'mei rabba....* May he bring peace upon us...." I remember listening to everyone in the sanctuary chanting alongside us and not realizing that I would be saying that prayer many times over the years. Although my grief would leave me always on the edge of not being able to utter the words, they would calm me.

On the way to the cemetery in the limousine, some black humour emerged, about how we were now the official *shiva*-sitters. Someone said, "You mean *shiva*-shitters," and we laughed, even Mommy.

Then *shiva* at our house; but this time it would mean something. All those others were rehearsals for this one, because it was my father, not some relative whom I hardly knew and for whom we offered our house. For seven days, there was a *minyan* at home where prayers were chanted, morning and night. Much food was brought over. Uncle Jonas was there and miserable Aunt Ada and the Hamilton relatives, and Daddy's sister Bessie and her children, and dozens of my parents' friends, and my sister's friends, and even some of my friends dropped by. There was a constant flow of people. It was all meant to support the bereaved and help dull the pain before reality set in and loneliness would consume the widow.

Mommy stayed upstairs a lot of the time in her bedroom. Nothing consoled her. Weak hearts ran in Daddy's family. His younger brother, Uncle Nat, had died of a heart attack two years before. Many years afterwards, I learned that Mommy and Daddy had been making love when Daddy's heart had burst. I couldn't begin to imagine how she must have felt when he died in her arms.

No one I knew at school had lost a parent, so I was different. Although my sister lived near us, I was alone in the house with my mother, and she was unbearably sad. I don't think she had any widow friends. She seemed to think that we had no money, and she went looking for a job. She had been a legal secretary before marrying, and before that, she worked in

New York at Saks Fifth Avenue in the handkerchief department—it was quite something in those days for a Toronto girl to go to New York. Still, the ideal then was to be a homemaker and have your husband be the provider, and she relished that role.

She found a position in a travel agency, although she resented being there as none of her friends worked. She didn't last long in that job. She missed my father terribly, and I heard her crying all the time. There was an enormous hole in my life, too, but she seemed oblivious to that.

At the best of times, Mommy was not a perky person and often fell into what I thought of as a sad mood. When her sister Sadie killed herself, Mommy was distraught, but it was all hush hush because Sadie had stomach cancer and had jumped from the observation deck of the Commerce building downtown. I was not involved in the discussions about that; I am not even sure when it occurred.

Mommy's ordered life as she had known it had fallen apart. My father was her focus, her sun. I do not know if there was insurance, but we were not destitute. My father did own all the Turofsky photo negatives, which numbered in the millions, along with his photography business and a building on King Street near John, which he'd bought a few years earlier. Our house was free and clear.

My home life had changed dramatically—no more music, no laughter, not much food prepared. Kraft Dinner became a mainstay; good thing I liked it, especially with ketchup. It is still one of my comfort foods. My mother said that she had to keep the house dark and cool to save money on electricity. She lost weight, and her skin turned a pale grey. She stopped going to the beauty parlour, and her hair became stringy and dirty. She never smiled and was always gloomy and depressed. The atmosphere was dismal. Any happiness that I had in my sister's bedroom was short lived. It meant nothing to me, and I started using my old room as a place to study. I even took to going to the basement to do my homework so I wouldn't hear Mommy weeping.

Every morning, I read Norman Vincent Peale's *The Power of Positive Thinking*. I have no idea where I had heard about it, perhaps on television, perhaps from a school counsellor, but I borrowed it from the library. My favourite chapters were "How to Create Your Own Happiness" and "I Don't Believe in Defeat". Then I went to school with a cheery expression on my face, pretending that all was fine.

My mother decided to take in boarders. One of those, a distant cousin, had a heart attack and died soon after he moved in. He was whisked away somewhere, I assume by the funeral home, and there was no *shiva* at our house. I didn't see his body and didn't feel anything for him: To me, it just happened. I was numb still from my father's death. I think his name was Leonard.

Another boarder, Lorette, a woman with wrinkled crepey skin, who smoked and smelled of formaldehyde, killed herself. I have no idea how. I thought it had something to do with the formaldehyde, but most likely it was pills. She was a strange person. I was living in some other world, as there was always a tragedy brewing after school at home. I grew accustomed to people dying, if that is possible. My home, which had once been a haven of security and happiness, became a house of strangers and bizarre happenings.

Our final boarder was Jean, in her late twenties and pretty in a tough Israeli sort of way. She was small and wiry, with a neat figure, short dark brown hair, and dark skin, with bluish numbers inside her arm from a concentration camp. She must have been very young when her family escaped from Romania then moved to Israel with so many other fleeing Jews. The details meant very little to me, although I knew about concentration camps. She did manicures and aesthetics. I believe she had been married and was divorced. She was friendly to me and brightened the mood in our gloomy house.

Mort hung around, a good friend and a shoulder for me to lean on. I went to a house party with him and heard some of the kids talking about me as "the girl whose father died". I decided never to go to another one. I just hunkered down to my studies, played some sports, and delighted in the arrival of my nephew.

Jordan was born about a year after my sister's marriage. I went to the hospital with Carol and Bernie, and it was a marvelous miracle, especially after our nail-biting ride down University Avenue, all of us certain that the baby would arrive in the car. Jordy was born very quickly, a blond blue-eyed beauty. I loved him so. I still do, fifty years later, and he is not only still beautiful, but he is also witty and thoughtful and shares my habit of making puns that amuse only us.

Even after Jordan's arrival, my mother remained miserable. Certainly, this was unnatural for a first grandchild's birth. She was in her own world, and ended up spending time in and out of a psychiatric hospital in Guelph, Homewood—an awful name. It was over an hour away and my sister visited her every Tuesday and Thursday, though I don't know how she did that; I went with her only a few times.

Mommy further lost interest in looking after herself. She stopped bathing and eating, and there was a strange odour when she walked by. I was getting used to her incessant crying and lying in bed, staring out the window. I just went through each day, studying and reading my Norman Vincent Peale, trying not to think about my father or our life before he died. It was over a year since he'd passed, and I knew I couldn't bring him back. But I was unable to convince my mother to move on, or to become optimistic again.

Of course, my sister and her husband were present in my life. She supported me and, when Mommy went *away*, I assume it was my sister who placed me in Aunt Ada's home, but I am jumping ahead in my story.

My mother showed little love for Jordan Louis Slatt, named after my father, Louis Joseph. This amazes me, now that I have my own darling granddaughters and am enthralled with them. Mostly, she seemed obsessed by some terror and, when it became overwhelming, she went to Homewood. I think my sister and Bernie must have made the arrangements, but I can't remember or don't want to remember. I believe she tried to slit her wrists before I came home from school one afternoon to find her with hankie-wrapped hands, but again I am not sure. Even now, I can't bring myself to ask my sister about it, as it is such a horrid vision. I became good at blocking out misery. Perhaps if I went into therapy, it would all come back, but who wants that? Writing about it is more than enough.

Each time my mother stayed at Homewood, I lived at other people's houses, because Carol and Bernie had a small apartment, and I was considered too young to stay at our house alone. Once, I stayed at a woman's place near where Mort lived. I think she and her husband had been friends with my parents, or Mort's. They probably thought they were doing a good deed by taking me in. They did everything to make me feel unwanted. When I played their recording of Frank Sinatra's "Come Fly with Me" and sang along, they told me, "Rickey, please don't play that album anymore and please don't sing." I always put the record back carefully in the white paper envelope and cardboard cover. Maybe they didn't think I should sing while my mother was in a mental hospital. I didn't stay there long.

Mommy was released for a short while. She would laugh when she talked of her best friend at Homewood, a Mother Superior, of all things. They joked together about a Mother Superior and a Jewish woman being friends. Apparently, she took to calling her Mom. I was relieved that my mother still had her old sense of humour. The next time she went away, I moved in with Aunt Ada and Uncle Jonas, who must have been in their late fifties or early sixties. They lived in a very nice neighbourhood opposite a ravine, just off Bathurst north of St. Clair in an area called Cedarvale. The house, decorated mostly in pale green with cold hardwood floors, was not inviting.

Ada was a commerce graduate from university, rare for a woman in those days. She was smart, frugal, and a lousy cook, except for the incredible lemon meringue pie she trotted out at family gatherings. I loathed those relatives because they were awful to us. Uncle Jonas was in the paper business, selling toilet paper and tissues and other such things. I guess my mother asked for some on one of her home visits, and they just flung it on our front porch like it was garbage. They didn't even ring the doorbell. It was so demeaning.

When I stayed with them, I watched them counting their money and putting it in bundles held with elastic bands, which they stored in brown-paper grocery bags. This was how rich people were supposed to live?

They treated me like a servant. I ironed the tea towels and Uncle Jonas's shirts; I did learn how to do this properly but detest ironing shirts to this day. I was rewarded with marvellous meals of canned wax beans, boiled potatoes, and some unrecognizable meat. They ate the same disgusting food, but I guess it satisfied them. It certainly wasn't about savouring flavours, and there were none of those lemon meringue pies.

Even though she's been dead and gone a long time, I still can't forgive Aunt Ada. I can't think of anyone else who ever instilled such hatred in me. I recently spent an afternoon with her youngest son, whom I hadn't seen in over forty years, after he found me on Facebook. I could barely look at him as he bore a strong resemblance to his mother, and I could only think of her during our conversation. I didn't like him much either.

In my vague memories of those visits Carol and I made to see our mother at Homewood, is the smell of disinfectant that seems endemic to all institutions. I detested the small airless bedrooms and cheerless common areas. I didn't want to look at the other inmates/patients because I feared what I saw in their haunted eyes. Writing about it now is very difficult and, even though it is a fuzzy memory, it still holds much sadness and a strange longing for me.

Little Miss Power of Positive Thinking had blocked out the wretchedness of it all. It is better to remember our past good family times, I told myself, and not think too much about the present. Perhaps that's why I still live in the future. Sometimes, I miss fully enjoying the present, but looking forward and planning ahead seems to be my modus operandi. It is my way of surviving. I think my sister likes living in the future and planning events, but she is much better at living in the present than am I.

The last time my mother was released, things were starting to look promising for us. Her appearance was good, and she was extremely upbeat. She smiled and seemed very focused. She was invited to a concert at O'Keefe Centre for an Israeli function. She dressed up in her jewelry and best clothes. She wore rouge and lipstick and had her hair done. I wondered how she would feel going out for the first time to an event without my father. She would see all the rich Jewish women and their husbands, but she went with a determined and happy look on her face. I was delighted to stay home with our newest boarder, Jean.

I was a teenager and longed to have someone listen to me and laugh with me. Jean was used to listening. She also confided in me that she was dating a very nice rich man. She eventually married him, and I hope she lived happily ever after.

When my mother returned from the performance, she sat and talked with Jean, showed her the jewelry she wore, and then gave the pieces to her. I don't think they were very special, and I certainly wasn't interested in them, but some weird alarm went off in my head.

The next day, I told Mort that I felt that something wasn't right. My mother seemed strangely content, doling out things to Jean, and I had this scary empty-stomach feeling. He suggested that I get in touch with my mother's psychiatrist, so I called him immediately. "You shouldn't worry. Sounds like your mother is getting things together. Learn to handle it by yourself," he said. After all, I *was* seventeen.

The next day I tried studying *Hamlet*, but I just couldn't keep my mind on the play. I kept sensing that something was wrong, because my mother wasn't at home. I thought that maybe it was the darkness of the play that filled me with a dreadful premonition. Then the phone rang, and I had to run downstairs to the phone nook on the main floor to answer it. "Is this the Turofsky residence?" "Yes," I said hesitantly.

"CBC Radio here. Can you tell us anything about the accident downtown at the Commerce building? A woman, whom we believe was Ruth Turofsky, jumped from...."

I threw the phone down and started howling. I had known something horrible was going to happen, and it did. The doorbell rang and wouldn't stop. Police. They had been sitting outside in our driveway, waiting for Jean to arrive home from work. They didn't want to tell a youngster the horrific news. When they heard my wailing and sobbing, it was evident that I somehow had found out, and so they rang the bell.

Two years, one month, and seven days after my father died, on November 21, 1961, my mother died.

My sister arrived, beside herself, but managed to take over and organize all the funeral details expertly. She was twenty-one at the time, and went to the morgue alone. I can't believe that my brother-in-law didn't accompany her. The *shiva* was at our house, and my girlfriend Maureen Silverman came over and washed my hair, hoping to make me feel better. It did. I will never forget that act of kindness.

People arrived and whispered around me. They brought food, but who wanted to eat? I just wanted to go to sleep and wake up to find it was all a nightmare. I hated seeing relatives like Aunt Ada and Uncle Jonas, so ignored them. Bernie gave the impression of being in control. He was twenty-eight, and seemed very mature to me. My sister was preoccupied with details, but it really is all a blur.

I was ashamed of what my mother had done and angry with her. I assumed everyone else was aghast and shocked. It was so selfish. It meant that no matter what was pulling her to that end, I was not important enough to keep her from killing herself. I was furious with that stupid uncaring psychiatrist, and I never heard from him. I was miserable. I was bereft. I was forsaken and wounded.

Even now, over fifty years later, it is painful writing this part. I am trying to get through it as quickly as I can, but I know it must be told, and the tears that are splashing on the computer are making it very difficult. I just couldn't figure it out, and there was no note, not one that I ever knew about.

I understand that my mother was sad and depressed, and guilty about my father's heart attack. She obviously felt there was no future for her. She did have to be brave to jump off the top of one of the tallest buildings in Toronto. She had to be desperate. She must have gotten the idea about the Commerce building from my Aunt Sadie, who had done the same thing years before.

I found out that there was an observation area on the thirty-second floor of the Imperial Bank of Commerce, as it became known after some merger. It was quite a tourist attraction and must have been easy to access. It was obviously not difficult to climb on the ledge and jump. I never went there, nor will I ever go, even though the building still stands. I can't imagine the scene, nor do I want to. It is all horrible.

Mommy and Auntie Sadie weren't really close, but the idea must have stuck in Mommy's head. Who knows? How do you explain suicide? Maybe she thought that I would marry Mort and be rich and looked after like Carol, or maybe she just thought that I was a survivor and could cope. Maybe she didn't even think about me. But how was that possible? She didn't even think about my sister or her grandchild? She must have been consumed by her own misery.

I swore I would never do anything like that, no matter what happened to me in life.

The newspapers wrote about all the gory details because of my father's celebrity status, and because it was dreadful news. The journalists left me alone. I am not sure about the rest of the family. We destroyed the articles. My sister and I wanted it all to disappear, to vanish from our minds. We rarely talked about it and still don't. It is too painful. No one talked about it to me. The funeral and burial were at the same synagogue and cemetery as for my father. My parents are buried together. My sister and I make certain that flowers are planted there yearly. We share the cost, but she spends more time there than I. I spend my cemetery hours elsewhere now, but that part of my story is still to come.

After this horrible loss of my mother, I realized that, at seventeen, I was an orphan. And everyone who knew me was aware of this sad fact.

Chaconne—Many Changes 1961–1965

After *shiva*, Bernie went looking for a place for me to live. My brother-in-law, already an accomplished doctor, was travelling to the top hospitals around the world in his chosen field of neural ophthalmology. There was no possible way that I could live with Carol, Bernie, and Jordy while I completed my education. Bernie visited our Rabbi in the hopes he might have an idea about where I should live, but Rabbi Rosenberg did not have any suggestions, nor any interest in helping me. Maybe he knew how much I disliked synagogue.

I had done my time at Aunt Ada and Uncle Jonas's house, and I certainly didn't want to go back there. They were the executors of my parents' small estate and my legal guardians, so money would be tough to get. No other relatives were approached about taking me.

Bernie went to my school principal, Mr. Mosey, who suggested that John and Frances White might take on a boarder because Sally, their daughter, had recently married. He said they were good people and would understand what I had been through.

The Whites were Gentiles. I once had a secret boyfriend, Art, who wasn't Jewish. Other than him, my only close association with Gentiles was exchanging Christmas gifts with the families who lived across the street on Wembley Road. I knew all the carols and could sing them with the best, and my father had had numerous non-Jewish friends because of his sports connections. The thought of living in a Gentile house was intriguing and scary, but I had no choice.

John White taught geography at my high school, Forest Hill Collegiate; Frances White taught the slow learners—what they called kids with learning disabilities—at Forest Hill's North Prep Elementary school.

They agreed to take me in, a Jewish teenage girl, because they knew my boyfriend and liked him.

Mrs. White had taught Mort in grade seven, and he was unique and intense. He drew a map of the world on the wall of her classroom with all the rivers and mountains. Every detail. He would go to school at seven in the morning. Mrs. White would go then, too, and encourage him because she was that kind of teacher, and he needed encouraging.

I sat opposite the Whites for my interview with them. For some reason, Neil Perkins, their son-in-law, sat on the sofa, while they asked me questions and told me about the house and my place in it. They lived at 303 Chaplin Crescent, just south of Eglinton Avenue. Most of the houses on their side of the street looked the same—red brick with narrow driveways. They are all now gussied up, as this area has become quite fashionable in Toronto.

I was dressed in my school clothes, a skirt and cardigan sweater—no pants were allowed in those days—and I was very nervous. Both Mr. and Mrs. White had greyish hair. She had a fragile build, while he seemed tall and sturdy, with a little bend in his posture. They looked kind.

"You don't have to stay in your room, Rickey. Feel free to use the whole house. Sasha will most likely want to sleep with you on your bed," Mrs. White told me. Sasha, their Abyssinian cat, was stretched out on the mantle over the fireplace and staring at me with intense yellow eyes. I anticipated the prospect of sharing my bed with a pet. This was a good sign. She continued, "In due time, we'll work out any small chores you can do, like helping with the dishes." No one I knew had automatic dishwashers in the early sixties. "Do you have any questions?"

"Can I have some fresh egg whites every night before I go to bed to put on my face?" I had read somewhere that would help my acne and make me beautiful.

She smiled. "Yes you can, dear, and feel free to join us watching television anytime. Mr. White is a hockey fan, but we also like *Perry Mason* and *Bonanza*. Lorne Green, a Canadian, is in it, you know." I did know because his twin sons were at my school, and we all knew that he was divorced and living in Hollywood.

The Whites' house was less than a ten-minute walk to my high school, so no more morning bus rides. Mort was encouraged to come over. After my move to the Whites, he was still very much in the picture as my boyfriend. He had stuck with me through all the bad times, when I felt like a pariah.

Mort was already in medical school, writing perfect exams, and examining cadavers. He wasn't so bad, and he didn't judge me. I could invite any other friends over if I wanted. The Whites knew my best friend, Carol Kirsh, because she had been at North Prep, and they liked her. Carol, whom I had met in junior high, still remains a good friend.

"What do you like to eat?" they asked. I don't remember what I answered. Although I was being interviewed, the Whites had already agreed to take me in. This was more like a get-to-know-you meeting than a trial. It was decided I would pay them ten dollars weekly for room and board, and I should move my things into their house as soon as possible.

I was anxious to get the eggs on, get to my new room, and go to bed, and to see if the cat really would join me. I don't remember if I had any clothes to unpack, or anything else for that matter, or even if I had brought the Norman Vincent Peale book. I just remember the stupid eggs and Sasha. She slept with me, and I loved it. I am still a weakling when it comes to pets sleeping in my bed and taking over.

Although apprehensive, I was relieved to get started in my new life at their home. The details remain sketchy. I don't remember actually leaving my beloved house on Wembley and walking out the door. I do remember that it wasn't sold yet, and all the furniture and piano were still there. I knew that was to come, but assumed my sister and Bernie or Ada and Jonas would deal with it. I didn't think about that, just about moving forward, and starting a new unfamiliar life at the Whites' house, and continuing at high school, and hiding my shame at my mother's suicide.

The Whites' house was much smaller than mine had been. When I came downstairs for breakfast that first morning, I noticed a table and three chairs in a small alcove and assumed it was used for breakfast. This room looked out on a compact garden beyond which was a train track. The narrow kitchen was toward the back of the house. Upstairs was one bathroom and our bedrooms close together. The basement had a ping-pong table, but I didn't see that until much later. The living room had a real working fireplace, cozy wine-velvet furniture, and the television. Their house was warm and welcoming and, before long, it became my home.

The Whites had a country cottage about an hour outside of Toronto, near the town of Orono in tobacco country. It was constructed of cedar, and they referred to it as the Farm. In the spring, we went there on weekends; in summer, we stayed longer. There was no running water or electricity at that time, and our food was cooked on a wood stove, with evenings spent playing Fish and Hearts and talking about Marilyn Monroe's death.

Mrs. White made simple meals at the Farm, with buttered vegetables fresh from her garden and home-baked berry pies on that wood stove. Everything was delicious, and I had a voracious appetite. Food has always played an important part in my life. I believe it is a symbol of warmth, love, and caring. I didn't know that then; I just sensed it, and I was always hungry.

Once I ran and ran in the woods until I was lost, and Mr. White had to find me. That made me feel like a very young girl who was cared-for, protected, and worried about. Perhaps I got lost on purpose. I waded in the icy-cold stream and let the sun warm me. I felt free.

As I write this, I get a lump in my throat thinking about the Whites' unselfish compassion. How lucky I was to land in such a place. I started to realize this fact as time progressed and I became part of their family. They made me feel that way. They weren't huggers, but their warmth was apparent when we said goodnight. I could perceive their happiness in my happiness. I could see their joy when I was joyful, at even the small things like winning at a game of cards. Did I just say lump? Now the tears are flowing at the memory of those special kind caring people.

I learned how to help out with small chores and felt good about myself. I slept well. The Whites had friends near the Farm, where we would visit; discuss the weather and the beavers that made a mess of the property; and pick up fresh eggs. For a while, I was going through them at a great pace, and then I reverted to just eating them.

Some of their friends were farmers, and some were other teachers. I was affectionately teased. I was very literal; when they would say something and pretend they meant it, I would take it seriously, and they would make me laugh when I "got" it. I started to feel happy and at ease. I would fall into bed at nine o'clock content and wake early to the freshest smells of nature and coffee brewing. I belonged.

I quickly became acquainted with the Whites' family. Their daughter, Sally, was friendly, agreeable, and kind. Her husband, Neil, was a music teacher and pianist, who possessed a wicked sense of humour. It is hard to describe examples, but he would say something that was ludicrous, and then a smile would creep across his face. There was Auntie, who was tiny and ancient, or so it seemed to me, and who had lived at the Whites' house at one time. Never married, she was a fixture in the family.

I experienced my first Christmas with them, even though they were adamant about respecting that I was a Jewish girl. One of their neighbours sent over the *New Testament* in hopes of some sort of influence, but Mrs. White would have none of that. In fact, she went out and found a menorah for Hanukkah at an antique store and gave it to me. It was exactly like the one my mother had, very old and made of dull brass. I still use it, lovingly remembering its origins. It brought back memories of Hanukkah candle lighting when my parents were alive, and it was placed on the breakfast-room table. We would take turns lighting the candles. My sister has that menorah now.

I hadn't yet accepted the deaths of my parents, not really. I just seemed to be living in a different life without them, perhaps away somewhere. It took years for it all to sink in. I would dream that they were alive, but I stopped saying my nightly prayers. I was angry at God because, even though I didn't *accept* their deaths, I knew on another level that they truly were dead.

After my father died, I thought that no more bad things would happen to me and I felt safe. But my mother's death ruined that. I didn't start to mark the anniversaries of their deaths for a few years. My sister did, going to synagogue and saying *Yahrzeit*, which means literally year/time, but actually is a time of remembering the dead by reciting the *Kaddish* or prayer for the dead, and lighting a 24-hour candle. I didn't started lighting a candle for my parents until I was married and had my own home.

The Whites encouraged me to take the baby grand piano from my mother's house, that was being sold, and we stuffed it into their small living room. My sister took most everything else of sentimental value, sterling silver flatware, silver service pieces and the like, ornaments, dining-room table and chairs, small tables that I recognize when I visit her home now. I gave a large Queen Anne wing chair to the Whites, who gave it to Sally. Strangely, I didn't want anything. I was young, and didn't care then about material things. I kept thinking how meaningless they were. Now I think differently. I value greatly what I have.

We usually spent Sundays with Neil and Sally, who came over for dinner. The table would be set with a lace cloth, good china, and silver flatware. We had well-done roast beef with gravy and loads of different vegetables, and a homemade dessert. Mrs. White's butter tarts and fruit pies were yummy melt-in-the-mouth treats with Crisco crusts. The smells from the kitchen and food preparation tantalized me during the day. Ravenous, I could hardly wait until six o'clock when we would sit down and say grace. It was Christian, but with no mention of Jesus Christ. In my mother's house, we had said the blessings in Hebrew before Friday night dinner and during Jewish holidays over the bread, the candles, and the wine.

Mrs. White brought out her worn copy of Handel's *Messiah* and started me singing again. On Sundays, Neil brought over his *Gershwin Songbook* and, after dinner, he'd play the piano, and I'd sing. The two of us would just take off and make music. I loved "Someone to Watch Over Me", "Summertime", and "But Not for Me", and just about anything in the album.

The music just flowed out of me, and my heart was full of joy. It was almost like singing back in my childhood home, with the family gathered around. After the music, we set up the card table and play crokinole or cribbage. I giggled uninhibitedly, loving the fierce competition of everyone, and noted the warm smile on Mr. White's face. I think he just revelled in my happiness and the fact that he and Mrs. White had something to do with my healing.

I cherished those evenings, and still treasure the memories of the chilly winter nights, with the fire crackling in the fireplace and all our laughter ringing throughout the house. I allowed myself to be happy. Their living room reminded me of covers of *Saturday Evening Post*, and I was just some sweet carefree girl who belonged in the picture. How I miss that particular camaraderie! It was harmonious living there but couldn't be compared to life in my parents' house. It was just different.

Most weekday nights, after I did my homework, Mr. and Mrs. White and I watched TV together. One evening I rushed out of the room when an episode of *Perry Mason* showed a woman jumping off a building. All of a sudden, I saw what it must have been like for my mother, and I couldn't believe that she actually did such a thing. My father would have been astounded that I was left to fend for myself and to deal with all the sadness and shame, too. It all came crashing down on me, and I had to escape to my room and cry. The Whites felt awful, and I felt badly for them, but somehow, I knew they would understand how very raw I still was.

The dreams I had about my parents were all happy and took place in my home on Wembley Road. I still dream about that home. I never woke up in a cold sweat or was disturbed in my dreams by the image of the jump. I may have been distressed, but I kept it submerged deep inside me and didn't let it out.

In the spring, Sally lent me her long pale blue satin prom dress to wear to Mort's graduation medical ball. Mrs. White made it smaller to fit me and gave me elbow-length white gloves to wear with it. Though the Whites treated me as if I were their own daughter, Sally never acted jealous. She seemed truly happy for me even when Neil said, "Boy, Sal, that dress never looked so good on you." He was only joking, of course, and Sally just laughed. It was that evening when Mrs. White said, "Rickey, if you like, you can call me Mother White, and Mr. White, Father White. That would please us."

It not only pleased me; I was over the moon. That same spring, Michael, the Whites' first grandchild, was born. He spent much time at our house, and I enjoyed the delights of yet another baby boy. This one was a redhead.

Mother White was a very patient tireless woman, and Father White sat with his pipe and a grin and seemed to enjoy all the activity around him. There was never a raising of voices in that house. When Mother White wasn't pleased with something, she would lower her voice so you could barely hear her, but you knew she was angry.

I remember a phone call she had with Aunt Ada, the hated one and my legal guardian. I was wearing my sister's hand-me-downs, and Mother White felt that I should be able to buy a few new clothes as I was going to start university. Ada wouldn't budge, and Mother White was livid. She just couldn't believe the stinginess of the woman. I had never seen Mother White so indignant, especially as she only asked for a small amount, about forty dollars.

Mother White was very protective of me, and Father White did the spoiling. How nice that was! The first morning after I moved in, I went down to breakfast and sat in their tiny alcove. Years later, I learned that I took Mother White's seat, the one she'd been using for over forty years.

Aria- song of a life

No one said a word, and that became my place. That's the kind of people they were.

I couldn't wait to finish high school. I had to complete grade thirteen, write my provincial departmental exams, and then I could start fresh in university, where no one would know my family history. I won a scholarship, so the money part for university was not a problem. The last year in school was difficult, because I was a Jewish girl in a mostly Jewish school, living in a Gentile home with a teacher from the school, *and* I was the one whose mother had committed suicide. I was embarrassed about my life. I was not popular, and was not invited to join a sorority, although I did have a few friends, including Carol Kirsh who stuck by me. I was an outsider who played bass in the orchestra, competed with the sports teams, and then went home to study.

It was 1962. Beach Boys music could be heard everywhere, but I preferred Peter, Paul, and Mary, and started learning all the songs from *My Fair Lady*. There was vague talk about a new group called the Beatles. The Cuban Missile Crisis was in the papers, but that didn't mean much to me. Jackie and John Kennedy were *the* beautiful couple. Mother White taught me how to read poetry and understand it by visualizing. Shelley's "Ozymandias" was the school poem of that era, and I nailed my final English exam because of her guidance, and because that poem magically turned up on the exam paper. Mother White knew all the subjects, and was impeccable in English and grammar. She loved teaching and was patient with me.

I found a part-time job at a ladies' store called Town and Country. I wore the store's clothes while I worked, which helped sell them. It was a great first job. I made twenty dollars a weekend, including Thursday nights, money that I could use to buy new clothes.

Mort was around. Although he had graduated from med school, he really wanted to be a forest ranger. His parents had pushed him to be a doctor, and he was a good son. But he was still very strange. His uncontrollable habits were getting more frequent—repeating phrases and tapping his forehead rhythmically. Sometimes he howled like a coyote. It was very annoying, and he couldn't stop. I would mention it to him, but he would continue his mutterings. He didn't seem perturbed by it, as he was almost in a trance when he did these gestures and noises. Although it was very noticeable, people just ignored it. We guessed it was a result of his being hit by a car when he was a baby in a carriage and sustaining a concussion. As I mentioned earlier, it was in time diagnosed as Tourette syndrome. Mort was also a great athlete. So, except for the shaking and muttering and the breaking of glass windows, we had stuff in common.

I learned about Foster Parents Plan on television and decided to adopt a child. Mort agreed to join me in this venture. It cost less than ten dollars a month, so it was manageable. He would pay, and I would write to our child every month. We began this when I was in university and continued for many years. Her name was Nguyen Thi Jacqueline, and we received pictures and progress reports. In fact, we were supporting her whole family. Our small sum enabled her to go to school. She had a disability: I think it was called torticollis, which made her head tilt. She was very pretty and wore pajamas all the time. I liked the feeling of doing good deeds. Mother White said, "If you help others, you will forget your own troubles. There is always somebody worse off than you." A statement I would never forget.

My world was expanding at a great rate, and I embraced it. That fall of 1962, I entered the University of Toronto in an honours arts course called Soc and Phil, Sociological and Philosophical studies. I'm not sure why I chose that course. It was a toss up between that and physical education. My brain won out over my body. I particularly liked philosophy because it challenged me, and because a brilliant, bearded very cool professor—whose name I have forgotten—taught the small tutorials. In those tutorials, I had my first experience of debating topics that centred on Socrates and Plato.

I still lived with the Whites and continued working at the clothing store. I joined the university choir and sang my heart out in a very pure boy-soprano way. We toured to Peterborough, a small town in Ontario, about an hour and a half from Toronto, and gave a concert there, a moving performance that was recorded.

I stood in the centre of the front row on the altar of a glorious modern church, with the sun streaming through stained-glass windows and lighting my face. I was infused with that adrenaline rush of singing in front of an audience. It was a very spiritual concert, although one incident on that trip was disturbing. When some of us were eating lunch together at a long table in the banquet hall of the church, one of the baritones started to make offensive remarks about Jews. I surprised him when I said, "By the way, I'm Jewish, and I'm insulted by your disgusting comments."

It was a daring moment, and I could feel my face burning, but I liked myself for speaking out. The Whites were helping to restore my self-esteem. I had only encountered anti-Semitic remarks once before when I was in elementary school. They came from a close friend. We had a fight about something, and she called me a dirty Jew. I almost laughed because of her mixed heritage, but the words stung. Living in a Jewish community, I was fairly protected and was always proud when I heard about Jewish people accomplishing great things and rising to prominent positions in the worlds of business and education. The arts were always filled with Jews. I never encountered anti-Semitism in my career.

I spent part of my Christmas holiday that year in Boston with my sister, Bernie, and little Jordan. We had such a good time. In fact, my sister and I always found a laugh, even when things were at their darkest. Carol planned a get-together with some relatives who lived there. She loved entertaining.

The walls were thin in Carol and Bernie's place, and I could hear them having sex in the middle of the night, or that's what I thought the creaking noise followed by sighs was. I was glad they were in love.

When they moved to Chicago a year or so later, they rented a house with a yard, got a boxer called Harry, and tried to train him at the same time they were toilet-training Jordy; I found myself stepping over poop, giggling, and attempting to guess who would be trained first. I visited when Carol graduated from Northwestern University and threw a party: The tradition of celebrations had begun for the Turofsky sisters.

One spring day during that first year in university, Mort gave me a very large flawless diamond ring. I was a bit surprised that he just went and bought it, but I guess it seemed the right time to get engaged. I was nineteen, he was twenty-three, and we weren't getting any younger. In the early sixties, you just didn't wait around. Marrying him would have pleased my mother, because she had promised him I would. Did I care about pleasing my mother? I was less angry with her and starting to see that she had unknowingly paved the way for a different sort of life for me, one in which I was thriving.

It was a choice of a June wedding or going to the summer course at the prestigious Banff School of Fine Arts to major in bass violin and minor in voice. After examining my options for about ten minutes, I chose the ring and the exhilaration of being engaged. My sister had married at nineteen, and so would I. Mother White tried to coax me toward the Banff option.

She liked Mort and knew him well, but I think she knew that I didn't have a clue as to what married life entailed. She was right, of course, but my young mind was made up.

At the university, an English professor became my mentor. He taught the Shakespeare class, and I used to meet with him after the sessions to discuss my work and toss around ideas. I flirted a bit with him, being very attracted by his London accent and style. He was kind of cute for an older man. He was perhaps thirty-one or two. *His* name I remember. I proudly showed him my new diamond ring. "I'm engaged and going to get married in June," I beamed.

"Are you crazy? You are, how old, nineteen? That's a ridiculous age to be getting married. It will end in divorce, I promise you. You can't possibly know what kind of man you will want in ten years. I assure you that this is wrong. If you want to bed someone for the first time, then do it, but don't get married." Somehow he surmised I was a virgin. So many of us were in those days, in high school and on into university. There was no pill, and we were taught to save ourselves for marriage. Maybe I had that look. He never quite came out and said, "Come to bed with me, ducks. I'll show you the ropes." But I had the impression that, if I had wanted to, he was ready to be my private tutor. It probably would have been an eye-opener and might have changed my haste in getting engaged and married.

I wore my sister's blush-coloured bridal gown, which had looked beautiful on her a few years earlier, but was too big for me. Someone had tried to burn down the synagogue a week before, so we moved to another one north of the city that wasn't as nice. The hubcaps on Mort's car fell off on his way to the ceremony, and he was late. Bernie gave me away. I had three bridesmaids, all in blue, including Carol Kirsh, and my sister Carol was matron-of-honour. It was a put-together affair, but I was so focused on the thrill of getting married and going on a honeymoon that I didn't dwell on the *real* sorrow of the moment—that my parents weren't there.

My sister planned it all expertly, and I think that she and Bernie paid for it. I cannot remember which relatives were there. Carol had been pregnant at the time, but lost the baby the weekend before. Still she managed to show up with a smile. None of this bode well for the young couple.

The wedding wasn't horrible; neither was it marvellous. I walked through it. I do not remember dancing or what we ate. Jordy, with his

Aria- song of a life

beatific face, wore a little navy suit with short pants. Mort's parents were very small and stubby. Mort's brother, Elliot, whom I liked very much, was smoothly tanned and handsome. He enjoyed a rich man's son's lifestyle to the fullest. He excelled at personal sports, like waterskiing on one foot and driving his motorboat very fast. He smoked and drank, and was charming and loving to me. He had a soft sexy playful voice and was always smiling. He was not good in school and lazy about it, the antithesis of Mort.

The Dorans had adopted Elliot and Mort as part of a war-baby program called *Open Your Hearts*. Jewish orphans were allowed into Canada under the terms of a unique federal order-in-council. I never warmed up to Mort's dad, Joseph, a Manchester immigrant married to Bertha Lipson. Her well-to-do family was in the garment trade, and Joe was an astute ambitious young man who helped build not only the McGregor Happy Foot sock empire with the Lipsons but also his own fortune.

Most of the celebratory event remains muted in my memory, except the wedding night, which turned out to be a revelation. Both Mort and I were virgins. I had been to a gynecologist who advised me to get some penis bottles to stretch my vagina. What, you might ask, are penis bottles? They are glass bottles of graduated sizes that looked like see-through penises. I actually needed a prescription to get them, and the K-Y jelly. Can you picture anyone wanting to buy them illicitly on the street?

There I was at the Whites with my package of pristine containers, purchased at a medical-supply pharmacy. I somehow told Mother White what I had to do. She just looked amused. The cat sat with me and watched me fumbling on the bed. One of the tubes was huge, larger than a milk bottle. I couldn't imagine that it was possible to get that in me. At any rate, every night I carefully inserted each bottle into the proper place, starting with the smallest and moving right along, preparing myself for the real thing. *Who would have thought?* I had never even used a tampon. I felt very ready for sex before my wedding day, but Mort wasn't tempted.

After the wedding dinner, we departed for the big night. We were booked at the Park Plaza in downtown Toronto, but Mort just wanted to drive around and around Queen's Park Circle. "What are we driving around for?" I asked impatiently. "Let's go to the hotel." My sister had bought me a beautiful peignoir with a pink sheer nylon negligee trimmed in beige lace, complete with a flowing matching robe, and I wanted to wear it.

Our room was very small, certainly not like the honeymoon suites in the movies. There were twin beds! Mort didn't want to change that, so I was glad we were both slim, because I was determined to see if the penis bottles worked. I hadn't actually seen a male sex organ before, except once, very briefly, in school when one of the boys was shoved naked out of the locker room. He was fat and ugly, and I thought his thing was disgusting. I never masturbated. I didn't even know the word in 1963, although I am sure others did. For me, sex was a mystery to be solved. After much fussing around, we did it. In. Out. Finished. Sticky. I liked it a lot, even though it was as basic as can be. It felt good. I slept well.

The next day we started on our honeymoon in the blue Pontiac Parisienne. We went to Vermont and Laconia, New Hampshire, home of the bestseller *Peyton Place* that was all the talk at the time. I sang along to "Moon River" on the radio and then "Tammy". I had one thought in mind while we were driving, and that was to get to the first motel and continue what we had started the night before.

I saw a small place called Shangri La, and urged Mort to stop early. I had plans. I didn't know what it was called at the time, but in that overheated motel room, with the faded oriental prints on the walls, the thin chenille bedspread, and the dripping faucet, I experienced what I later learned was an orgasm. Yowee! Again, the act was as basic as ever, but what a finish.

I didn't want to sightsee or drive around. Just get me to the next motel, and I was a happy girl. Mort, on the other hand, was not as keen; in fact, he wasn't interested at all in stopping early every day. He just wanted to drive fast.

Before we married, we had petted quite a bit, nothing heavy and never touching below the waist, but Mort wasn't aggressive or very interested in sex. He was even a bit prudish. I wore a bikini when they first came out, and it was modest by today's standards. He actually did not want me to be seen in it. I was fourteen. The short time I'd tried dating other boys, I did more with them than with Mort. He was waiting to be married.

After a week, the honeymoon was over, we headed back to our newly rented apartment on Castlefield Avenue, and I returned to my second year at university. Morty was an intern at the Toronto General Hospital, and I, a newly married woman, invited other young doctors and their wives for a meal, and started to learn how to cook and clean. Carol, Bernie, and Jordy returned to Toronto, and I spent much time with them. I had the piano moved from the Whites to my new place and chose a bright green silk-brocade chesterfield and matching chair for the living area and teak furniture for the bedroom. I was set.

Mort's family supplied us with plenty of money from all sorts of investments in his name. They even had put some in my name, probably for tax reasons. They owned many buildings on University Avenue and the sock company. Mort earned little as an intern, but we lived well for a young couple. I never regretted moving from the Whites, and I saw them as often as I could, along with Sally and Neil. I didn't care about the sex. It was regular enough, and we still did not know that he had Tourette syndrome, so I didn't attribute his disinterest to that. He worked long hours and slept at the hospital and was always tired.

I kept singing with Neil, who became adamant that I audition for a colleague of his at the Faculty of Music in Toronto, as he thought I had real promise. They sent me to George Lambert at the Royal Conservatory, who had been the voice teacher of the famous tenor Jon Vickers. Mr. Lambert gave me a few singing lessons and tried to convince me that I had talent and should get serious about it.

That November, John Kennedy was assassinated, and the world changed. I spent time with the Whites watching the events of Lee Harvey Oswald unfold on television. It was two years and one day after my mother's death. Somehow the two events were connected by horror and sadness.

Mort decided we should move to the Yukon, where he would be a practising doctor. The forest ranger in him was pushing its way to the surface. I had no choice but to go along, especially as he'd been offered a job in Whitehorse in a medical practice with hospital privileges. I am not sure how I really felt. In the early sixties, a wife did what her husband wanted. I had to give up university, my Toronto friends, and my family. My excitement about singing didn't enter into the discussion. Mort knew I had talent, but it was unrealistic to even consider it as a career possibility. His future beckoned. I followed. I could hardly wait to leave sophisticated Toronto for the wilds of the north. Sure.

Riki Turofsky

Mother and Father White, Sally and Neil Perkins circa 1962

Riki and Neil making music for the first time 1961

Aria- song of a life

The wedding party 1963

Divertimento—New Adventures 1965–1967

One beautiful July day, Mort arrived home, with a newly purchased red Peterborough canoe tied to the roof of a newly purchased dark green Mustang. "What is that?" I demanded. "That's our canoe for the Yukon River," he said proudly. "Yippee," I replied unenthusiastically.

The investments we had from his parents made us financially very stable, which meant we could easily afford a canoe, but who wanted one? We packed up the apartment, put everything in storage, and took off on our cross-Canada adventure, headed to a new home five thousand miles away, with a canoe on the roof of our car.

On a hot summer day, dry and dusty, we arrived in Whitehorse in the Yukon Territory. Most of the streets weren't paved because the intense cold in winter would make them heave, due, I was told, to the permafrost. When the roads and everything else was frozen, you could hear cars coming from blocks away—creaky, crunchy, crispy sounds. There were no stoplights, and only a few grocery stores with very basic, but expensive, food, because it was transported to the north from a great distance.

Hougens Department Store carried everything you needed in clothing and furniture. Murdochs, a jewelry store, sold, among other gems, little silver spoons with gold nuggets fashioned into the shape of a caribou mounted on the tip. I still have some. About five thousand people lived in Whitehorse, ten thousand in the entire Yukon Territory. It was a transient society of nurses, social workers, and teachers there for isolation pay, as well as doctors, lawyers, and dentists who cherished the northern life for their families.

A smart residential neighborhood called Riverdale was where most of the professionals lived, and where we eventually moved. The affluent lived there, but the natives living poorly elsewhere. At that time, the

Yukon had the highest rate of alcoholism and suicide per capita in Canada. Not many murders, but wild dogs running in packs would occasionally attack little children.

Significant Whitehorse buildings included: a library, a school, a hospital, one really good steak house, a hotel of sorts, one television station, the government-owned CBC, and Robert Service's famous cabin. Service was renowned for his poetry, and Canadian schoolchildren memorized his famous "Cremation of Sam McGee", which I can still recite. Little had I known that I would be living in the land of the midnight sun when I first learned it. Social gatherings abounded, and I learned how to party in Whitehorse.

En route across the country, probably around Dryden, Ontario, I started to worry about what I was going to do in Whitehorse, as there was no university and little else as far as I could tell. So I decided to get pregnant. I didn't formally announce my plan, but I stopped taking the pill. I didn't tell Mort immediately, because he probably wouldn't have wanted a child, and I wasn't going to risk that. The pill was pretty new then, and no one was sure but it was said that you could get pregnant really fast if you took it and then stopped.

Initially, we moved into a furnished rental apartment in which every suite was identically decorated in colonial-style furniture covered in blue nubby upholstery, no elevators, no view, just grimy downtown streets outside the window. It wasn't long before I lost my normal appetite and began to have a serious craving for pumpkin pie. I guessed I was with child.

When I told Mort, he seemed happy enough. He really was preoccupied with his new job and working long hours. Fortunately, I had a terrific new friend and next-door neighbor, Lorna MacIntosh, who could make a mean pumpkin pie on demand. "Lorna, I need pie with vanilla ice cream on top," I begged. It arrived and I gorged.

Lorna made me laugh with her sardonic sense of humour and voice to match. She had wavy reddish hair, a pointed nose, and freckles, and was slim. She was nine years older than me and the smartest person I had ever met. It was great to have a pal who lived so close.

She and Jim, her dentist husband, were in love and full of joy. I was envious. We spent a lot of time with them. They teased Mort mercilessly about things like showing off his slides of our trip and repeating pictures of mountains, over and over. Mort loved big scenery. He hardly ever included people in his pictures, even though I liked those photos the best. They didn't say much about the coyote runs at night, when Mort would howl at the moon. This, of course, was another manifestation of Tourette syndrome. We still didn't know he had that unusual disease. He would bundle up and go for a run at night—this *was* the Yukon after all and pretty frigid—and he would howl. He couldn't help it; nor could he help uttering obscenities. He would shake and fidget most of the time, but when he was operating or dealing with patients, he managed to control the compulsive behaviour.

Everyone in our circle of friends was older than me, but full of high spirits. They were doctors, lawyers, judges, and businessmen, and their wives, all of whom were warm and welcoming. A sponge, I soaked up their northern knowledge, along with advice about my pregnancy. I was invited to drop in any time for a coffee and conversation at their homes. I did this often because there wasn't much else to do during the day and I enjoyed my new female friendships.

Socials, beginning with six-in-the-morning phone calls, were one aspect of my new Yukon life. "Whatever you're doing, it's Thanksgiving, and we're having a breakfast get-together. Get out of bed, and get your sorry butts over here now, and come exactly as you are," demanded Bill Buchan, a Scottish doctor and head of the clinic.

I was in a flannel nightie, and Mort in striped pajamas. We put on our coats and did what we were told. When we rang the doorbell, Bill and his wife, Nicki, greeted us with Screwdrivers and Bloody Marys. She was wearing a long fancy gown, and he was in tails. It was seven in the morning. The mood was set. The party lasted all day, with masses of food and hilarity and, at some point, dancing and banjo playing. The usually very reserved Nicki sang "Dixie" with her American accent, while high-stepping around the room.

Snowmobiles, as we know them today, had just arrived in Whitehorse. Our terrain was perfect for them. We would hop on, go for a wild ride through the woods at night, and then have dinner at a Dutch-owned steak house, where they served garlic bread and baked potatoes, a fashionable meal at the time.

We celebrated Klondike Days. The men had to grow beards after New Year's as part of the festivities or else go to a phony jail that was set up downtown. During this festival, people would come from all over the territory to compete in different games, dogsled races on the Yukon

River, and gambling. We wore long dresses in the style of the late eighteen hundreds, that were available in abundance at one of the churches.

There was no synagogue in Whitehorse. Apparently, one Jewish man lived there, but he wasn't religious, and no one seemed to know him well. Morty's mother was quite concerned about this deficiency in our little city. Although I had rejected the formal part of being a Jew, I always embraced the cultural aspects—the food, the holidays, and some of the traditions. Before Passover, I asked my mother-in-law to send up some *matzo* and *gefilte* fish, as well as some prayer books. I hosted a dinner for our friends and made a Rickey-style *seder*. Everyone seemed to enjoy the exotic delicacies.

In summer, we paid midnight visits to our neighbours, crawled in their open windows, and jumped on their beds to surprise them. It never was really dark, so we just stayed up with them and played. The winters were long, with the night arriving early in the afternoon, and things were pretty quiet around town, except for the sounds of babies-in-the-making.

In Toronto, I had never drunk much of anything except Mateus rosé; in Whitehorse, I learned to like whatever I was given, and sampled saké, with its powerful unexpected effect. Our friends were well travelled and urbane, even if we weren't. One fall, they ordered oysters flown in from the Maritimes. I had a chance to try my first raw ones—strange slippery little creatures that I still adore. They imported wines from France for their cellars, which also held a variety of foreign after-dinner liqueurs.

One unusual party paid tribute to the Beatles and Mary Quant, and all the women wore mini-skirts and go-go boots we bought at Hougens. An old claw-foot bathtub was filled with booze. I could have stayed all night, but Mort wasn't very social, not interested in dancing, or not having that kind of good time. We left with the apology that he was on call at the hospital later that night.

Although we were still so young, our marriage was one of convenience. His crazy tics and mutterings constantly annoyed me, and there certainly wasn't any fire in our relationship. We had a bond of many years together. I was twenty-one and he twenty-four, and there was no passion, just comfort—ridiculous for a couple of our age. We were more like brother and sister than husband and wife. We got along, laughed and explored, and rarely quarrelled, but there was no spark. I was pregnant though not particularly interested in sex, and we never discussed our sex life. I hardly remember how often we made love. We certainly weren't creative—just the missionary position, no foreplay, no after play. I never talked about sex with Lorna. People just didn't discuss private things like that; at any rate, I didn't.

We were invited to the RCMP ball, a very formal evening and *the* event of the season. I purchased a magnificent tangerine gown with a low-cut jewelled bodice and flowing chiffon skirt—no chance that anyone else would have that dress as Hougens only bought one of each style. When we arrived at the hall, we were given tiny sterling silver spoons embossed with the RCMP crest, that I still have. A full-course fancy dinner was served, and we danced not only with our husbands but also with the Mounties in their complete regalia. Nothing quite like dancing with a man who has spurs on his boots, and trying to avoid injury. Mort introduced me to a young couple, close to our age. He was an officer in the regiment, and she a nurse at the hospital. Peggy, with very blond short hair, was slim and perky and I was to remember her for a long time.

Even though I knew the baby would keep me busy, I was bored when we arrived in Whitehorse. I found a used out-of-tune piano for sale and decided to give lessons to the children in town. I urged Mort and Jim to bring the piano up to our place on the third and top floor of the building. It was a very old heavy upright—those things weighed well over eight hundred pounds—and the guys struggled and swore as they dragged it up the stairs, while I laughed hysterically. As it turned out, I hated listening to the mess the kids made of the music. I had little patience, so that venture ended quickly.

I had brought my autoharp with me from Toronto and sang folksongs at the library for small audiences of children and their parents. I was very busy, trying to keep myself busy. I even purchased a broom and took up curling, not witchcraft, although that might have been more exciting. And we went canoeing, once. Thank goodness for the morning sickness excuse.

I made my own maternity clothes on a sewing machine from the Sears catalogue, having taught myself how to make wearable outfits—if one didn't look too closely at the seams. I couldn't follow a pattern so I improvised, and Lorna helped. Tent dresses were in fashion. Everything was crooked, but the materials were chic. If I sneezed, the things would fall apart, so I didn't sneeze. I joined a theatre group and starred in *Snow White and the Seven Dwarfs*. I was a very pregnant Snow White and, when I sang, "Some day my prince will come", my friend Jim, who was a huntsman in the chorus, shouted, "He already did." It wasn't the most professional show, but everyone loved it.

Our first winter in Whitehorse was frigid, minus 50 Fahrenheit for over two weeks in February, my birthday month. We had to plug our car in. We couldn't stay outside for long, or we would get frostbite. I bought long underwear, a parka with a fur-trimmed hood, and mukluks. The cold was crisp with ice fog. Amazingly, I didn't seem to feel the cold because it was so dry, and I had my big belly to keep me warm.

I read an abundance of books, including Theodore Dreiser's *Sister Carrie*, and decided that was a perfect name for my daughter, having assumed I would have a daughter. No ultrasound tests in the Yukon then, just monthly weigh-ins, so it was just a guess. At this time, I changed the spelling of my name from Rickey to Ricki. I was tired of people thinking that I was a boy.

We travelled the summer of '65 to Dawson City, about 400 miles north of Whitehorse. We had an emergency kit in the Mustang and extra tires because it wasn't *if*, but *when*, you would get a flat on the unpaved gravel highway, and we had many. We always picked up hitchhikers, because we might be the last, or indeed only, people for hours on the road. The mountains were rugged and awesome, and the lakes cool blue. I will never forget the majestic beauty of those jagged mountain ranges. Everything was so dry that the car was always covered in dust, as were we. Even my tongue was furry.

The restaurants on the highway were few and far between, and I mean far. They were simple diners, with no menu and only one offering—usually some homemade soup or succulent stew and freshly baked bread. A Crispy Crunch chocolate bar would be dessert. Our conversations with the owners revolved around the dust, the highway, the dust, the local wildlife critters, the dust, where we were going, and where we were from.

When we finally reached Dawson, we noticed that it wasn't much changed from the pictures we saw of the Gold Rush days in 1898. We visited an old folks' home and talked with the residents to try to absorb some of the gold-fever history. We stayed in a musty-smelling hotel, which has now been restored into a replica of a brothel, called Bombay Peggy's, and sells a lot of Macallan scotch to help pass those long summer nights. I stayed there a few years ago on a return nostalgic visit and sampled the scotch, but that is another story.

On one trip, we ventured to Alaska on a narrow-gauge railroad, ate freshly-killed moose on the way, stayed in a decrepit rooming house with a rusty claw-foot bathtub and not much hot water to fill it, and wandered the empty streets of Skagway. There were no cruise ships disgorging thousands of passengers then. We went to Valdez, the only port in the north open year round, where they fished for king crab and canned it. We woke at four in the morning and waited for the clouds to lift off the top of Mt. McKinley, the highest peak in Alaska, so that we could see the famous Dall sheep that roamed there.

In the winter, we visited glaciers and snowshoed, even into late March. That was when the baby dropped really low. Although I wasn't feeling the cold, I did miss the warmth of my childhood winter Florida trips. I learned that there were charter flights to Hawaii from Whitehorse and thought it would be a great idea to go. It was important to get *outside*, I reasoned, or you would get what they called *cabin fever*. So I booked a trip, when Mort had a week's vacation from the clinic.

We left minus 50F weather, landed briefly in Vancouver where it was plus 50F, and then to Honolulu for plus 80F. By this time, I was eight months pregnant and had to dig a big hole in the sand to lie in the sun on my tummy. We ate teriyaki steak, listened to Don Ho, and visited a classmate of Mort's, Brian McGrath, who was doing his doctoring in Hawaii. He was married to a California-type blond with a perfect body. I was a frump beside her; even without the stomach, I would have been a frump beside her. She was movie-star material. She wore a minuscule bikini and, as hard as I tried, I couldn't find any flaws. Damn. On top of this, they lent us their Chevy Corvette convertible to drive around the coast. Nice people, too. Unfortunately, Mort had an accident: No one was hurt except the car, and our relationship with them.

I had Carrie on April 6, 1966. I wanted her to be born before Aubrey Tanner, my doctor, went to Hong Kong on a long trip, so I drank cod liver oil. It was ghastly, and nothing happened. Then I drank castor oil, and that did it. Most everyone had babies by natural childbirth in Whitehorse, and I was no exception.

The native women just squatted in the snow, had their babies, and didn't make a sound. I had an easy delivery, but not in the snow, thankfully, and I made a lot of noise. Carrie just slid out. Maybe it was the oil. Aside from her red hair, my darling baby daughter looked just like Mort, especially when one of the nurses put a pair of little glasses on her.

It was a special place, Whitehorse General, painted pink inside and out, and there were only two other women on the maternity floor when I was a patient. I was fussed over, not only because my husband was a doctor there, but also because that was the way they were in a small town. I pranced around in my pink wedding negligee and had *schvitz* baths. I stayed for seven days in a room filled with flowers. It looked out on Grey Mountain and the city, a calming vista. I delighted in my baby, who weighed well over seven pounds. I called my sister in Toronto to announce the good news. Carrie Ruth Doran, my precious redhead named after Sister Carrie and my mother, Ruth. I guess I had started to forgive her.

I breast-fed Carrie, not common in those days, or so my sister told me, and I had no home help. There wasn't even diaper service. I didn't use disposables, because they were still pretty new on the market and very rough. So I washed all the smelly diapers in the basement of the apartment house. I spent my days walking around Whitehorse with Carrie's pram, dropping in on friends and chatting, reading novels, eating, and doing laundry.

Mort didn't seem to be interested in Carrie or in me, for that matter, and he was very cranky when I made noise in the kitchen cleaning up. He worked most of the time, or so I thought. When Carrie was about nine months, I took her to Toronto to visit hern grandfather, who had been ill. I can't remember exactly what was wrong, but I think it included a short hospital stay, and I thought it would cheer him. And it would be a welcome change for me. Mort was working full out in the hospital, and it was a chance to visit my sister.

Mort's mom was ecstatic on seeing Carrie; his father was not interested, but she was only about nine or ten months old. We had a pleasant visit; after all, I had known them for over nine years, so I felt at home in their presence, and they had a modern new home with a large grassy front lawn. It was very green, totally opposite to Whitehorse's rugged exterior.

Mort called. In 1966, a long-distance telephone call was uncommon and brought good news or bad. "I think you should know that I am seeing Peggy," he said quietly. "You remember, she's the nurse who is married to the Mountie. I introduced you at the ball."

"You're what?" I stammered.

"I seem to be involved with her, and I thought I should let you know, before you come back and find out."

"Damn right!" I shouted and hung up the phone. *That little bitch.* I remembered her vivacious figure and blond hair. I was angry at Mort, but I blamed Peggy for enticing him. I couldn't wait to get out of Mort's parents' house. It would have been very hard to tell them that their son was having an affair, so I didn't. I hadn't planned to stay there more than a week, and my leaving was not unexpected.

Because I knew I could ask anything of her, I called Sally to see if she would keep Carrie while I went to meet Mort to try to save our marriage. Fortunately, I had started to wean Carrie, and she had taken easily to the bottle, so that part would not be a problem. I was hurt, jealous and angry, and determined to show that little vixen, Peggy, that I was the one Mort loved. I suggested to him that he meet me halfway in Edmonton. I bought a periwinkle-blue soft wool suit, a dress with matching coat, and for some reason, I had my honeymoon/baby-birth negligee with me. I assumed that dressing up would do the trick.

Edmonton was numbingly cold in January, even colder it seemed than Whitehorse. I was shaking most of the time, but that might not have been the weather. We stayed at the Chateaux Lacombe hotel and booked a meeting with a marriage counsellor. We both were interviewed for about a half an hour—about our feelings, about Mort's girlfriend, but it was really all surface talk, no probing, and a fair amount of tears on my part. Then Mort said, "I really like Peggy, but I love Ricki and Carrie, too. I'm not quite ready to work things out." The marriage counsellor idea was a flop. Even though I was wearing the new blue outfit and had worn the negligee the night before, Mort didn't even notice.

We headed back up to Whitehorse, stopping a few times to let passengers off, as it was the milk run. Carrie was still with Sally in Toronto. I cried and vomited most of the way back and lost my self-worth around Prince George, about three quarters of the way. Mort mostly slept. The stewardess was very kind, when I told her that my husband was having an affair. I was not sick, just upset. She left me alone in the tiny bathroom. When we finally landed after about ten hours of flying, I couldn't wait to get home and try to think things out rationally.

We had recently rented a Riverdale house owned by a long-haul trucker, who lived in the basement, but we mostly had the place to ourselves. When we arrived, Mort disappeared outside to check the car's plug-in battery and the snow around the house, and I went into the kitchen from the side door, opened up the refrigerator, and found dog food. We didn't have a dog. Neither did the trucker. I then went to Carrie's room and found soiled sheets in the baby's crib that weren't hers, but ours, although I had nothing to do with soiling them. I was wild with indignation and immediately called Lorna to tell her what had happened.

Mort seemed to be in his own world about his relationship. He was really liked and respected at the hospital and by his patients, but he was way out of line here. I don't think Lorna was surprised when I related all that had transpired. She liked Mort well enough but, more than anything, she was my good friend. She hushed me, speaking in an unruffled voice, "You must calm down and compose yourself. I was married before Jim to another man. It didn't work out, and we divorced. It happened long before we came up here, and I've kept it a secret, because we know what people think of divorce. Look how well my second marriage has worked out. Just thought I would let you know that."

If Lorna could have such a great second marriage, then there was indeed life after divorce. That solved it for me. It never took me long to make a decision, and divorce was quick and easy in the Yukon. I immediately phoned my friend Erik Nielson, well-known in Canada as Yukon Erik, who was a member of parliament and a lawyer, and hired him. I found Mort lying on the sofa in the living room. I was holding a glass of orange juice. When I told him I wanted a divorce, he responded, "That's ridiculous."

"Are you going to give up Peggy?"

"I really like her, but I love you." I couldn't figure out his fascination with her, except that she was new and different from me. I threw the glass of juice at him. "Get out! You can sleep on the couch until you find someplace else. You have till tomorrow."

I knew that he couldn't stay in the house, as that might look as if I were still sleeping with him and condoning his relationship with Peggy the nurse. In 1967, the divorce laws were very specific about correspondents, persons who were accused of having intercourse with the spouse.

Everyone in Toronto, except Mother White, thought I was crazy to get rid of a rich doctor husband, instead of just overlooking his wandering. Mother White was quite adamant in her views. "Never stay with a man who has strayed from his marriage. It will eat away at you. You will be happier on your own."

I arranged to meet Sally in Edmonton, so that I could pick up Carrie. We had been separated for more than a week, and I missed her terribly. Much of that time and the travel is hazy in my memory, but Carrie seemed fine, if a little hollow-eyed after her cold and the plane travel. Sally would have given her much loving care.

Mort wanted to share the lawyer, but he had to get another one, albeit at the same law firm, there being few choices in a small town. The *decree nisi* was granted within a few weeks of my decision; the *decree absolute* within a month. Peggy was named as correspondent, and Mort agreed to a small alimony. His parents sent many papers that I had signed for some of their companies and asked me to remove my name. I assumed it was all about money.

In fact, they thought I should get very little to support Carrie and myself, suggesting fifty dollars a month, even though they still owned McGregor Hosiery and a good deal of University Avenue in Toronto. I didn't understand it, but I didn't care. I was just anxious to get on with my life. I asked for five hundred dollars a month, and they agreed. It was a good sum that would help look after us, although not what I could have asked for and received.

The night of my divorce, an old friend from Toronto, who had recently come up to Whitehorse to work as a doctor, took me out to all the bars to celebrate. I saw my first go-go dancer and mingled with some of the younger crowd who lived in town, people close to my own age. I had a ball.

At one party, I met a very attractive social worker, who suggested that I might need some therapy after the trauma of divorce. He offered to provide it. A few nights later, after trudging miles in the snow from his place across the bridge over the Yukon River, he arrived at my house, his beard frozen with ice crystals. As I watched him undress, I started laughing, because it was taking ages for him to get to his long underwear. Not quite like in the movies, but he seemed to know a great deal about love-making, and his therapy worked; my self-esteem was restored. I learned that the missionary position wasn't the only way for a girl to have sex.

On February 21, 1967, the day after my twenty-third birthday, I was divorced and living in the Yukon with my adorable ten-month-old daughter. The day after that, I found myself standing on the tarmac of the Whitehorse airport in minus 40F weather. My facemask, parka, mukluks, sealskin mittens, and long underwear didn't help much. I was part of the meet-and-greet committee of the Yukon Concert Association in my newly elected position as vice president, my latest keep-busy project.

I was waiting for the Canadian Opera Company to arrive for two days of performances in the high-school auditorium. February in the north had to be the most bizarre month for visiting artists, but nevertheless oddly exciting.

You could never get lost at the airport, with only one or two flights a day. Luggage arrived fast and frozen, and it was easy to find visitors. The singers were obvious, with their necks bandaged in scarves. There were orchestra musicians, clutching their instruments; some young guys in jeans, who were probably stagehands; and some middle-aged folks, who must have been dignitaries—all from Toronto. As they descended the stairs from the plane, they looked tired, cold, and miserable with that "what-am-I-doing-here?" look on their faces. I found my specific charges and whisked them off to the Whitehorse Inn, the one hotel downtown that was almost presentable.

The next night was the performance we had all been anticipating—the event of the winter season. The opera was *Don Pasquale*. The stars were Jan Rubes, a bass with a booming voice, who was utterly at ease and commanding on the stage; and a soprano, Gwenlynn Little, who was cute and sparkling. I was captivated and thought *I bet I could do that!* I knew I could sing, but accompanying myself on the autoharp in the Whitehorse library and performing as a pregnant Snow White were hardly the prerequisites for becoming an opera singer. Then I recalled the singing teacher Neil had taken me to in Toronto, who said I had something special.

At the reception after the opera, I met the editor of *Opera Canada* magazine, Ruby Mercer. She told me of an initiative in Vancouver called the BC Opera Ensemble, a training program of the Vancouver Opera Association, for young artists. I was intrigued. Now that I was free to leave Whitehorse, it sounded very appealing. Maybe I should audition for the opera program and see what happened. Alternatively, I could go to university and study music there. I had played string bass and had that year of an honours arts course from the University of Toronto. Anything was possible. Perhaps my divorce was an opportunity for a very new kind of life.

Vancouver was the logical choice for my move because it was directly south of Whitehorse and definitely warmer. I didn't want to go back to

Toronto as a failed married woman with a baby. So my mind was made up quickly, as usual, and I decided to pack up Carrie and leave Whitehorse. A week later, Jim and Lorna took us to the airport. Mort had visiting rights whenever he wanted. It wasn't formal. He didn't seem to mind that we were leaving. Nothing was said, and nothing was in the agreement about moving. I don't think he even came over to say goodbye to Carrie.

As we were about to leave for the plane, Jim offered me some advice and a phone number on a small piece of paper. "If you have any problem finding a place to live, call my mother. She owns a boarding house in Kitsilano. I'll let her know you might call. You'll like her, and she will welcome you both."

Arriving in Vancouver, Carrie and I went with all our stuff to a business associate of Mort's father. We stayed only one night. He was a representative for my ex-father-in-law's sock company. Both he and his wife, although pleasant, encouraged us to leave.

I called Jim's mother, Helen MacIntosh, and asked if we could stay there. In her warbling voice, she responded kindly. "I'll get a crib at the Salvation Army store, and you can meet me at my home this afternoon after my chiropractor's appointment. Oh, and don't tell Jim. He hates chiropractors."

A taxi delivered us, along with all our gear, to her doorstep. Mrs. MacIntosh greeted us with, "Forget the rent. Put your money away. You're a friend of Jim's, and that's good enough for me to think of you as family." That was a promising start.

Vancouver was a visual dream, with its splendid mountains and spectacular views, especially after the frozen whiteness of the north. The house on West 1st in Kitsilano was one block from the water and the smell of the sea air. The crocuses in February, after the minus fifty temperatures in Whitehorse, were breathtaking. Fortunately, I had learned to drive a standard car in Toronto when I was first married. Once I had learned the vagaries of shifting gears, laughing hilariously as the car hippity-hopped down the street, it proved a valuable skill. I bought a used Volkswagen, which I called Linus, because I loved the Snoopy characters, and the car looked like it should be dragging a blanket.

Then we nested.

Roomers lived upstairs in the large old wooden house, with its huge front veranda, a typical Vancouver style. At the entrance was a vestibule, in which stood an ancient upright piano. Behind an etched glass door, the living room was filled with cozy sofas and arm chairs, all covered in pale blue velour. The adjoining room, along with a dining table and chairs, had a breakfront filled with knickknacks, reminding me of the Whites' house. The hub of the main floor was the large kitchen, with its high ceiling, yellow wood kitchen cabinets, yellow linoleum floor, and yellow dinette set, a happy colour, reminiscent of the breakfast room in my Wembley Road home. Beside the refrigerator, a back door led out to a small garden.

We slept in the basement. Mrs. MacIntosh moved into a renovated small bedroom down there, and gave me her garage bedroom next to Carrie, who was ensconced in the furnace room. There was a bathroom for us to share, with a cast-iron tub, and if I timed it just right, early in the morning, there was enough hot water for my bath. I bought a hose with a showerhead that attached to the tap, so that I could wash my hair. I managed most times not to soak the floor, as that contraption kept swinging out of the tub with a life of its own.

Mrs. MacIntosh had short soft white hair, wore glasses, and had smooth round cheeks. She explained that she had a minor form of Bell's palsy, so she seemed to be always smiling. She was a great old dame, happy, generous of spirit, full of stories, and a good listener. And she adored Carrie. Her neighbour, Elsa, a professional nanny, immediately fell in love with my little redhead and helped out with babysitting.

It was super talking with Mrs. MacIntosh We would sit for hours in the kitchen discussing the possibilities of my new life. She was delighted that I had a car, so we could drive all over the city. I was always getting lost, because I just couldn't figure out what was north in Vancouver, with the mountains and the water confusing me. Every day, I put Carrie in a stroller, and we walked to Kitsilano beach. The weather was glorious that first summer, and I was deliriously happy. I started calling Mrs. MacIntosh, Nanny Mac. She became a surrogate grandmother for us. We all laughed a lot, and I felt very fortunate with our new home and family

Riki Turofsky

Riki with dusty car and canoe in the Yukon 1964

Newborn Carrie in Riki's arms, Whitehorse 1966

A Capella—The Singer 1967–1968

It was time to get going on a career. I was, after all, twenty-three years old. 1967 was a big year in Canada with our hundred-year celebrations, and I considered my departure from the Yukon to be my own centenary project. I made an appointment to meet the head of the voice department at the University of British Columbia to see if I could enter the Faculty of Music there. He was extremely friendly and welcoming, but he wanted to put his hands all over me to see what kind of breath control I had rather than listen to me sing. Perhaps that's what was expected? I later learned that he was a very fine voice teacher, who could feel the breath through my diaphragm, but it distracted me. He was one of those very intimidating mesmerizing men, and I knew that Mr. Lambert at the conservatory in Toronto never did that.

I didn't think too much about my looks then because I was preoccupied with getting my life together, but I had a good figure—tall, slim, and curvy. My hair was cut short like Julie Andrews in *The Sound of Music*, and I didn't consider myself sexy or flirtatious. When I told Nanny Mac about my meeting at UBC, she offered advice. "I don't like the idea of that professor touching you, even if it is to see how you breathe. I think you should stay away from him."

I phoned the Vancouver Opera Association and asked if I could audition for their Ensemble program. I used Ruby Mercer's name, figuring they would know her. They asked me to come and sing two arias. We set a date.

They mentioned that there were a few single tickets available for *Lucia di Lammermoor* that night, part of the Vancouver International Festival, and I could buy one at a reduced rate. It was starring the world-famous

Riki Turofsky

soprano, Joan Sutherland, so I jumped at the chance. I knew little about opera, but had certainly heard of her.

While we were waiting for the opera to start, the man sitting next to me started a conversation. It was obvious that I was alone, and he was curious about why I was there. Today I often ask young people a similar question when I see them at operas. It turned out that he was Bjorn Hareid, president of the opera company. He knew all about the new Opera Ensemble. I told him I had just arrived in Vancouver and was going to audition. He wished me luck.

Joan Sutherland's singing captivated me. Her velvety voice filled the vast theatre, almost as if she had a microphone in her face. Her stupendous high notes seemed effortless, and her soft ones floated on air. When she finished the big sleepwalking scene, it was the first time I had heard such tumultuous applause. There was an immediate standing ovation at the end of the opera. With tears in my eyes, I knew that this was a once-in-a-lifetime experience.

I could hardly wait to audition. I practised with a recording of arias that I borrowed from the library. The singer was Anna Moffo, whose mellifluous voice I loved. I didn't have any sheet music, so I learned the arias by repeating the excerpts on the disc over and over. I am sure Nanny Mac was ready to sing the music herself. If I hadn't been in such a hurry, I probably could have found the music, but I didn't know where to begin that quest. I thought I sounded just like Moffo, and was full of confidence when I went downtown to the opera company's rehearsal building.

Entering the room, I wasn't even nervous. Having never been to an opera audition before, I didn't have a clue what to expect. I sang the two pieces I had memorized—"Cherubino's Aria" from Mozart's *The Marriage of Figaro* and "The Jewel Song" from Gounod's *Faust*.

Fortunately, the accompanist had the music, as it had never occurred to me that he would need it or expect me to bring it. When I entered the rehearsal hall, all I could see were two men at the far end, sitting behind a table strewn with papers. They asked me what I had chosen to sing, and I told them. I was wearing my royal blue wool dress with matching coat, the one that I had bought to save my marriage to Mort. After I'd finished the Mozart, they asked for the Gounod. Then one asked, "Tell us about your training."

What training? "I've just arrived from Whitehorse, where I heard the Canadian Opera Company on tour, and I thought that doing opera looked like fun and something I might be good at. I know I can sing and act, and I wanted to audition for your new Opera Ensemble." When they didn't respond, I continued, "I met Ruby Mercer, the editor of *Opera Canada* magazine at a reception up north in the Yukon, and she suggested that I might like to try to get in your program. I do have musical experience. I sang Snow White in the high-school auditorium, where the opera company performed. I have just gotten a divorce and have a ten-month-old daughter, and I have a nanny, and it was either this or going to university for a music degree. So here I am."

"Well," one of them said, "You certainly have a lot of nerve." I took that as a compliment. "You do have a natural voice and sing right on pitch, but we would like to see if you can learn two complete opera roles—Gilda in Verdi's *Rigoletto* and Mimi in *La Boheme* by Puccini. In one month's time, return here, and show us what you can do."

I was energized. They gave me the scores to take home. I went back to the boarding house and told Nanny Mac what had happened. I thought I was the luckiest girl in the world with such a chance. All I had to do was work very hard, learn what I had to learn, and nothing could stop me.

The old upright piano in the front vestibule was a bit out of tune, but no matter. I later found out that it was sharp in pitch by a semitone, a good thing for a soprano: If she practises singing sharp; then when she performs, the high notes aren't as high. For example, if I sang a high C, I was really singing a C#, which is higher. Then when I was in the studio and sang a C, it was a breeze, because it seemed lower. It was just a matter of placement of the notes, and because I didn't have perfect pitch, this didn't trouble me, at the beginning. As I progressed and developed as a singer, I knew that the note sung was not the note written on the page by the feel of it.

I set about to read the original stories of both operas and to learn the two roles. I found recordings at the library and worked tirelessly. I loved the music, and it didn't seem all that difficult to sing, especially the Gilda role, which just fell into place. I decided not to copy the singer's voice, like I did with Anna Moffo, and to just use my own. A novel idea!

One month later, I returned to the Vancouver Opera Company and sang through most of Gilda's part. I was alone with the pianist, Robert Keys, and I thought things were going pretty well until I began the second act. He abruptly stopping playing and left the room. *That was the end of that.* I had started gathering my things together and was ready to leave when he returned with the general director, James Norcop, who asked me to repeat a section I had already sung. The two men smiled, and Mr. Norcop said, "You need a singing teacher badly."

Oops, I thought. I guess that does it.

"We'll set you up with one, as well as a full scholarship. See you in class on Monday."

I flew out of the room. My hand was shaking so much, I could hardly fit the key into Linus's ignition. My heart was soaring. Could I even find enough superlatives to describe my elation? I drove home and raced into Nanny Mac's kitchen.

How great to have someone to tell. She was as happy as I, and we decided to celebrate, with dinner out at the White Spot Drive-In restaurant on Broadway. They had the best southern fried chicken and scrumptious burgers. Carrie couldn't talk much yet or walk, but I knew she understood "yippee" and "yahoo"! A full scholarship was amazing. I would be able to start looking for an apartment, and Nanny Mac could move back into her bedroom. My $500-a-month alimony/support (they were lumped together then) would pay for a place, food, and Elsa to look after Carrie. She charged $50 a week and did the cleaning as well.

I found a one-bedroom penthouse up the street from Nanny Mac's so I could see her all the time. No elevator, but it had a huge balcony and splendid view of the water. I recently went to visit my old neighbourhood. The apartment now has a splendid view of another apartment. The rent was $150 a month with all utilities. Food was $10 a week. I asked the store manager if a delivery service was available. It was, and it was free. With the little cash left from my parents' estate, I bought a used piano, that was just fine for practising.

I met my new voice teacher, Katerina Hendrikse, a very pretty and refined woman from the Netherlands. She had taught the excellent baritones Victor Braun and Cornelis Opthof, so I was very fortunate. After she heard me sing some of Gilda's aria, she told me, "Your voice is very clear, very natural, you sing on pitch, and your high notes are effortless. I can help you make a well-supported sound, with good breathing. You seem to have an innate sense of character and drama. I think you have charisma. This is going to be hard work, but we will have a good time together." The lessons cost me $20 for the hour, and I saw her every week. I still had over $100 each month left for other expenses.

I loved working with Mme. Hendrikse, and she with me. She was very protective of my voice, guiding me carefully through the repertoire for a lyric coloratura soprano. She made me sing Mozart. She told me not to drink tea as it dried the vocal chords, but to drink honeyed hot water instead, and keep away from air conditioning.

The classes at the Ensemble were demanding and stimulating. There were eight of us. All the others were experienced, having been to university where they had studied voice and performed. I was a neophyte. There were movement classes with a ballet master, Peter Franklin-White, from the Royal Ballet in London; acting classes; language and diction sessions; and singing with coaches like Robert Keys from Covent Garden, who had been the accompanist for my audition. No wonder he could make the piano sound like an orchestra.

I went home every night and drove the neighbours crazy with my practising. They must have loved us, Carrie with lungs of steel, who could cry with the best of them, and me, vocalizing into the long hours of the night. I worked as hard as I have ever worked at anything just to keep up with the others. I wasn't worried anymore about keeping busy. I had natural talent, a very good voice—almost as good as everyone else's, good presence, and a fervent ambition to be the best. I was focused on achievement and not wasting time. I had Carrie after all.

Every day, I would drive across the Kitsilano Bridge and soak up the incredible Vancouver view of mountains and sailboats floating on the waves. I'd find my way to the opera company rehearsal space on Richards. I was usually loaded down with music scores. When I walked in the front door, I knew that our resident director was there, as the place reeked of Brut, his cologne, the fashionable scent of that era. I don't think Steve liked me much. I certainly hated the way he smelled of perfume. He wore tight jeans, and had a reddish goatee that matched his long hair. His skin was pockmarked, but he was sexy in a swaggering sort of way. I felt he was suspicious of my talent and was questioning why I was there with the more accomplished singers. But he had to work with me, and I learned a lot of stagecraft and discipline from him. When he complimented me on some small thing, I was over the moon.

The first concert I participated in was held in the rehearsal hall, with an invited audience of donors and friends and a music critic, who wasn't going to be reporting but was just interested in the very new concept of an opera training program. We all sang together—no solos, just duets, trios, and ensembles. The repertoire included some obscure songs of Mercadante and Donizetti.

There was a mezzo-soprano, Judith Forst, with a rich flexible voice and brilliant high notes. There was a budding dramatic soprano, Lyn Vernon, with a laugh that rang out through the building as well as a marvellous singing voice. She was a single parent like me. There was a bass baritone, Steven Henrikson, who had a robust voice, was a character actor, and became my best buddy. Another baritone, John Duykers, had a dark beard, was very good-looking, mysterious, and sexy, and I was attracted to him. There were two more sopranos and a lyric mezzo.

I was still overwhelmed by being the new girl who didn't fit in. Robert Keys, the *repetiteur* or vocal coach, and Elaine Korman, his girlfriend, an accompanist and coach, played some duo piano pieces as well. Robert was an expert in *bel canto*—literally beautiful singing, but referring to an Italianate vocal style popular during the eighteenth century. It included impeccable legato, graceful phrasing, agile flexible technique with embellishments. Bel canto was having its revival thanks to Joan Sutherland and Richard Bonynge.

Our first concert was gratifying. I loved the applause. I don't remember being too nervous, just excited and a little shaky for the first few bars of music. Afterwards, the music critic from the *Vancouver Sun* followed me to my car. I thought he was going to tell me how well I sang. Instead he asked me to go for a drink. I told him that I had to get home to my daughter, and he said he would be in touch.

One other aspect of that evening of firsts stands out in my memory. I was wearing pantyhose. They had just come on the market. I loved the way they fit and didn't miss the garter belt. Didn't wear one again until years later, when I recognized how sexy they were.

My new life in Vancouver consisted of practising, learning music, going to class, and looking after Carrie. She was just starting to talk, and stumbling when she tried to walk, but she was adorable and fascinating. I felt sad that she didn't have a father around to be a male role model and Daddy-loving type, but it was what it was. She loved Elsa, Nanny Mac, and anyone I brought around. She was becoming pretty and starting to look less like Mort, which was a good thing. The combination of red hair, blue eyes, and tawny skin was unusual.

On a beach-stroller walk with her, I met Klaus, a German puppeteer. We would often see each other and chat. Nothing more. He didn't seem interested in sex. One Saturday at the beach, when we all went swimming, I noticed he had the hairiest back I had ever seen. Actually, the blond hair on his head was thinning. His back obviously had the bulk, and it wasn't blond. Men were not waxing their backs in the '60s, but he would have been a perfect candidate.

On a warm spring day in 1967, he took me to Mount Washington near Seattle and tried to teach me how to ski. We rented equipment for me: The boots were low-cut leather with laces; the skis were pretty basic. The snow was mushy, and I tried my luck on the beginner hill. I was doing quite well, when Klaus took me to a more advanced slope because he was bored. I fell. He insisted that I walk back to his car rather than get ski-patrol help, and by the time we reached the parking lot, my ankle had ballooned to fill my ski pant, throbbing and hurting miserably. Klaus wasn't interested in hearing about my pain. He drove back to Vancouver about two hours away, dropped me at my apartment, and told me to ice it. Lovely! My leg had blown up, so that I was forced to cut my ski pants off. I kept Carrie's sitter, who had been there all day, and took a taxi to the hospital, where I was told I had a broken ankle. An intern put a large plaster cast on my lower leg up to my knee and gave me crutches, and I taxied home.

I couldn't believe that Klaus had just left me on my own. To add insult to injury—now I knew where that expression came from, he never called, not even to find out how I was doing. Moreover, as part of the program at the Ensemble, we were supposed to attend the Vancouver Opera productions at the Queen Elizabeth Theatre, and there was a performance two days after the cast was put on.

Somehow, I arrived at the theatre and sat with the other students, including the sexy baritone. When the last-act curtain came down and I tried to hobble out on my crutches, my leg was so painful that he offered to carry me to his car, drive me home, and drag me up all the stairs to my apartment. So there I was, new to the opera studio, my leg in a cast, a toddler to care for who was just learning to walk, and living in a penthouse without an elevator. I also couldn't drive.

After a few days, I was still quite wretched when I noticed a blackish blue tinge around my toes that protruded from the cast. I went back to the hospital and insisted on seeing an orthopedic surgeon, not an intern. Ironically, the doctor who attended me was one I had known in Whitehorse, Jack Hibberd. He had just moved to Vancouver and was on staff at the hospital. He cut off the cast, which had been put on too tightly, and fitted me with a new one with a walking heel, and I was on the mend, as Nanny Mac said. Best of all I could drive. When I arrived home from the hospital, the sexy baritone came to visit and showed me how to take a shower by covering the cast with a garbage bag. He also insisted on helping me wash my back.

The Ensemble's first touring production was *Hansel and Gretel* by Englebert Humperdinck. Although this opera is based on the fairy tale and is meant for children, it does need strong singers in all the roles. We were performing with piano, but singing with a full orchestra would have been another matter. The orchestration is rich and heavy, sometimes reminiscent of Wagner, and would be too demanding for young singer's voices.

I was told that I would be singing one of the Gretels, so I started learning the part. It was charming, melodic, and childlike, but very difficult. Mr. Norcop was definitely not pleased that I had a broken ankle and was hobbling around in a cast. I wasn't pleased either, but I didn't tell him that. He informed me that in Germany the singers were not allowed to ski when they were under contract.

"I am certainly never planning to ski again, so no problem." I told him sheepishly. That didn't turn out to be true, but who had a crystal ball, that showed twenty years in the future? Fortunately, the cast would come off while we were still in rehearsal.

Robert Sunter, that music critic from the *Vancouver Sun*, whom I had met after my first Ensemble recital, called to ask me out for a date. I was looking forward to dating him as he was an older man of thirty-five, who drove a red Mustang and wore tweedy suits. He was about five foot ten, not tall, but I could wear heels, and he would still be taller. He had dark brown wavy hair, smooth white skin, curly eyelashes, and a chipped front upper tooth. He was very fit as he had played soccer in his youth and still played a bit. There wasn't any fat on him, and not much body hair. He was handsome in a Michael Caine sort of way (but not quite so good-looking), British, with a mid-Atlantic accent. He was an excellent writer, aloof and arrogant. I was enchanted. He knew everything about music, or so I thought.

Robert was feared and respected as a music critic, and confident and sophisticated about everything else. Over our first dinner, he began teaching me about wine and food. I was a sponge. After dinner, he invited me to see his place—an old musty-smelling apartment with a fireplace and a large paper lantern light in the dining room. At a very crucial moment in the evening, his nose started to bleed profusely—everywhere, including all over me. It was a total mess, and I giggled uncontrollably. He had to rush out to the hospital, which was neither sexy nor urbane. He finally returned, but the moment was lost.

We started seeing each other often, and Robert encouraged me to let my Julie Andrews hair grow. Wanting to please him, I began to do everything he suggested. I bought a blond fall to match my hair, like the extensions that are used today. No one would know it wasn't my hair unless they came to my apartment when I was washing it and saw it hanging outside on the balcony to dry. When I wore it, I was told that I looked like Julie Christie, and that made Robert happy. He told me what clothes to wear, and how to speak with a more modulated tone. He convinced me to get rid of Linus, my Volkswagen bug, and buy a Fiat 850 coupe in red, his favorite colour, which I named Faruggio—Italian car, Italian name.

Robert taught me about orchestral music, the ballet, and contemporary dance, and which restaurants were good and which were not; and he started signing his notes to me, Pygmalion, after the Greek artist who created a piece of sculpture that came to life. Was I really clay in his hands? I certainly was malleable at that time.

While he was dating me, he had two other girlfriends, one a dancer and one in the arts industry. In the beginning, I was happy to be on his roster, but before long, it drove me crazy with jealousy that he insisted on seeing all three of us. I never saw him with them, which was a good thing, but I did find out what they looked like.

At the Ensemble, I was immersed in developing the role of Gretel when another singer, Wendy Pollock, arrived from London, England, to share my role. I hated Wendy the moment I saw her. This wasn't easy as she was very nice, had a good sense of humour, was annoyingly tiny, and even looked like the part. Her English rose skin was perfect. No pimples at all, and I was still covering up occasional breakouts. Mr. Keys had known her in England.

After the recent acrimonious departure of the general manager and artistic director of the opera company, a new manager, John Findlay took over. It was said that Wendy and he were involved romantically. So she rather had an inside edge, I thought. I cried quite a bit with this turn of events, but there really wasn't anything I could do except strive to be a better Gretel than she.

I was given a bunch of Dew Fairy pieces to sing, as well as the few Gretels. The Dew Fairy had one aria that was very difficult and required dancing around the stage in leotards. I hated the role and was outraged at this turn of events, as only a young soprano could be. The dancing Dew Fairy had to wear ballet slippers, and I knew that real dancers covered their soles in resin so they wouldn't slip.

One of the stagehand's duties was to make sure that my shoes were safe. His name was Les. He was tall and craggy, and accommodating. Every night, after he handed me my shoes, I would do my running bit and feel quite secure. Years later, when I was singing at the Queen Elizabeth Theatre in Vancouver, where he worked as a stagehand, we reminisced about the tour, and the slippers. He told me that, in fact, he didn't have any resin, but just held the shoes and then gave them to me. We both laughed. Foolish singers!

Ironically, I became good friends with Wendy after she returned to London. We started to correspond. I even stayed in a room in her wild and riotous house in Herne Hill on one of my London visits. There were singers and pianists everywhere, with people running in and out of bedrooms in the middle of the night, much like an English farce. Memories of our Gretel rivalry faded quickly. We still keep in touch.

The *Hansel and Gretel* tour took us to dozens of small British Columbia towns I'd never heard of. We travelled by bus, and the whole cast and crew fraternized. We stayed in crummy motels, vocalizing and agonizing. If one of us got a cold, we all got it. There was much moving about during the night, with little assignations and some that were not so little. The tour was a success, and I even had a review for my first scrapbook—"charming interpretation, light clear voice and looks like Gretel."

Back in Vancouver, we did a double bill of Menotti's operas, *The Telephone* and *The Medium*. I sang in both, sharing the roles of Lucy and Monica. We performed these in the opera rehearsal hall to an appreciative audience. I was reviewed favourably once again. All reviews were encouraging and complimentary, and I happily lapped them up. How proud and delighted my father would have been that his daughter was singing opera.

Meanwhile the strange romance continued with the music critic. Robert prided himself on being a great cook, and hosted a dinner party, which featured roast pork with crackling. I arrived to find him *sans* eyelashes. He had stuck his head in his old gas oven to check on the meal, evoking memories of *Hansel and Gretel*, and somehow he was singed, losing what I liked most about his face, his long curly lashes. Fortunately, the dinner was saved; with the mouth-watering crackling that I still love. The lashes never grew in again.

I began to notice his imperfections, and dating a critic posed some problems, but I was still "mad about the man" as the song says. The other singers in the Ensemble were not as friendly to me any more, although they were not that friendly to begin with. If they received poor reviews, I felt they somehow blamed me. Robert was objective and overly careful when writing about my performances, which meant that I didn't get great reviews from him, even if I deserved them. I usually had very good ones from the other Vancouver critic, but Robert was the one in the city that mattered. I should have challenged him about this, but I was too insecure.

I continued soaking up knowledge from Robert about music and the composers, and his insights into the various artists who were performing. Often, he interviewed them a day or so before their concert, so he had opinions about their personalities, and I wondered if this ever informed his criticism of their performances. He would dash back to the paper after a show and write his review on an electric typewriter. There were no computers or emails, but Robert always made the deadline for the next day's edition.

I loved the musty aroma of the newsroom, the blend of tobacco, ink and dust. It reminded me of the nights when I trailed after my father to the newspaper offices, and he delivered his hockey photos. It was stirring and nostalgic, and I was falling head over heels.

Robert wrote well, with humour and a good use of the language, but he could be callous as well as complimentary. Everyone invited him to parties after the shows, and I often went along on his arm. The homes we went to in Vancouver were extraordinary, many overlooking the water of Howe Sound, and the people were erudite and cultured. Robert was fawned over, and we were treated very nicely indeed. Some people were even starting to recognize me.

When we went out, I dressed with a flourish in boutique clothes that weren't expensive but had flare. I didn't have a lot of money to spend, but I had a good figure and long blond hair—well, I owned it. I was young and full of life. I was told I was sexy, which is perhaps as much an attitude as anything else. Robert was very demanding about how I looked, aside from the long blond hair. He liked provocative outfits, and it *was* the '60s, so I complied. I did everything I could to win his approval.

Although I was seeing a lot of him, there was the matter of his two other girlfriends. I was still competing with them. It was challenging and edgy but horrible for my self-esteem. What self-esteem? I had worked so hard to restore it after Mort's departure, and now it was tenuous once again. It was disheartening to know he was with one of the others, when he was not with me. I was even starting to develop my stalker skills. Knowing where the dancer lived, I would grab Carrie and cruise over to that woman's apartment to see if his car was parked outside. It usually was when I suspected it, and then I felt awful. I was such a fool but couldn't seem to help myself, as I was determined to be the only woman in his life.

Robert was good with Carrie, which wasn't difficult as she was such a dear little thing and adored the attention he gave her. She was developing and growing, and I was busy reading my Dr. Spock and learning how to bring up a rambunctious two year old.

I planned a birthday party for her with some little friends and their mothers. Nanny Mac and Elsa came, as did Robert. Carrie wore a frothy powder blue dress. It was a sunny day, and our balcony was filled with toys, little doll baby carriages, and balloons. Carrie was entranced by the balloons, but I am not sure she really understood about birthdays. She loved having all the people around, almost as much as she loved our walks to the park and swing time there.

It was a hectic life for me, with classes, practising, performing, shopping, dating, and stalking Robert. But I was happier than I had ever been. I was always in a state of high energy, so different from the mellow days of Whitehorse.

And speaking of Whitehorse, Mort called one weekend, said that he was in Vancouver and wanted to come for a visit and take Carrie to Stanley Park. She was very happy about this, but he didn't show up for hours. She was so disappointed that I realized I could never trust him as far as making plans for Carrie. She did have a good time at the park though. She loved the attention and, even though she was so very young, she knew he was her father. Amazingly, and sorrowfully, he never brought or sent her any toys or anything until many years later when it was too late. He and I were civil. I was so exhilarated with my new life, I hadn't missed him for a moment. I was angry that he let her down, but it was good for her to get to know him. Strangely, I didn't ask him about himself. I just wasn't interested, so I don't know if Peggy was still in his life, and I didn't care.

The Metropolitan Opera National Council auditions were held every year, and all the Ensemble members were preparing for them. They took place across the country in February of 1968, and were the first ones in which I competed. I didn't quite understand the significance of these auditions, but I was told they were important. Mme. Hendrikse, my singing teacher advised, "Sing what you can sing well, even if it is not demanding, or showy. Be able to sing it in your sleep, or with a cold. No one is impressed with a difficult aria poorly performed."

There was an application process and preliminary steps, but the big concert audition was the highlight. It was thrilling. I wore a silky coral dress and high heels, and my new long hair was half up and half down. I spent a lot of time on my performance arias, and I felt prepared.

I sang Marzelline's aria from Beethoven's *Fidelio*. Although it was stirring, it wasn't a passionate or particularly taxing aria, but it was perfect for my young bright voice. There were a few spoken lines in German, that I said before I launched into the aria that set the scene. "*Da kommt Fidelio in unser haus, und seit der seit ist alles in mir und um mich verendert*" meaning "Then Fidelio came into our house, and from that time, everything in me and around me changed." I still remember those lines over forty-five years later—they were so ingrained. I let my speaking voice sound breathless and full of love for Fidelio, who was really Leonore, a woman, disguised as a man—the usual uncomplicated opera plot. I loved saying those words, as it was rare to speak in an opera. The aria was simple, and direct. I nailed it.

I was not exactly nervous, but very energized, which seemed to be my arousal state when I performed then, and throughout my career. I was able to put that excitement into the character of a young girl in love. We did these auditions in Seattle, competing against other Canadian and American singers.

Judith Forst was the star of the day. She won the auditions and a chance to compete in the finals at the Met in New York, where she had a contract to work. I also caught the judges' attention and won the Studio Award for the most promising artist. I won some money, a chance to join the Met Studio, and some glowing accolades from the judges, along with career advice. A letter from the auditions secretary dated February 24, 1968 gave me two of the judges' comments, "Her voice has warmth, and considerable potential beauty. Her style of singing indicates temperament, and some dramatic sense, excellent delivery showing solid vocal preparation, all this in one year. Wonderful! Tremendous potential." My first exposure to celebrity! The newspapers covered the event and featured our pictures. I felt that the audience responded to me. I experienced the power of the solo performer; my ambitions were set. I sometimes imagined that my talent would take me great places, but mostly I didn't allow myself to think of those things. It was enough just to work hard and go from day to day.

Later that year, I entered the San Francisco Opera Auditions. Judi didn't do these as she was on her way to New York, so I had a chance. I won the regional auditions in Vancouver, and my prize, along with money, was to be sent to San Francisco for a month, for the Merola Opera training course for young singers. I was grateful for the opportunity, and torn about leaving Carrie, but I knew she was in good hands with Elsa and Nanny Mac overseeing. I realized that I had to follow this career opportunity. I was in a different life from women my age, who had stable family environments with husbands who worked. My path seemed determined by fate.

The remarkable program began with full orchestra performances by all the finalists in the War Memorial Opera House in front of a large audience. I didn't win the grand prize, but the company had many requests from the newspapers for interviews with me. They seemed fascinated by my appearance, voice, and energy on stage. They said I looked more like a starlet than an opera singer, and they wanted to write about my life as a young artist. That resulted in a big feature in the weekend edition of the *San Francisco Examiner*, the beginning of all the press that I garnered during my career.

When I write about my looks, it's hard to be objective. I have been going through my old scrapbooks. The pictures and articles often referring to my physical attributes make it evident now to these older eyes that I was quite stunning, even beautiful. I did not realize then my full impact on the stage or in a concert. I knew only my shortcomings. I knew I was attractive, but Robert always pointed out my faults, the weaknesses in my appearance and in my singing. He was a critic after all. With his involvement with the other two women still continuing, my self-regard was rocky. I believe this is a common trait of many female performers, especially those with an influential older man in their lives, whether a lover, manager, or music critic. These mesmerizing men exert power over their young beautiful charges. Now, I know it was his way of controlling me. Then, I loved having someone tell me what to do. I strived always to satisfy him and never quite succeeded.

As part of our training that summer in San Francisco, we performed two complete operas with orchestra. I was chosen to sing what was to become one of my favourite roles, Musetta in Puccini's *La Boheme*. The performance took place at Stern Grove before ten thousand people. Additionally, I sang Papagena in Mozart's *The Magic Flute* at Paul Masson Vineyards. Things were moving along at a heady pace.

Robert Keys was hired as a coach, and we had Italian diction classes with a tiny demanding Italian woman, Signorina Colorni, who wrote *the* book on singer's Italian diction. She was so small that she had to sit on a table for us to see her. The lessons I learned in that class were invaluable throughout my career.

The part of Musetta matched my voice and personality. It was not difficult for me to sing, with my effortless high notes, and there were many of those in the score. It was a visceral thrill to soar over the orchestra in the big second act ensemble. In fact, it was thrilling to know I could be heard over all the other voices and instruments, because Puccini wrote it that way. It was a part that could easily steal the show.

Musetta was flamboyant and sexy but had a soft nature. I tried to find this vulnerability, so that she wasn't just a one-sided character, as she is so often portrayed. There is nothing quite like singing one of the most famous opera arias "Musetta's Waltz" and knowing I could do it without much fuss. I just had to open my mouth and let it happen. It was so natural for me.

It became my party piece, and I probably will still be able to sing it when I am ninety, although I don't imagine many who would consider a ninety year old a sexy coquette. I don't suppose anyone would pick me up and trot about with me on their shoulders, as happened in that production. Maybe they'd push me around in my wheelchair, and I could tantalize all the old guys at the seniors' home.

The aria is guaranteed to bring the house down, and it did. The costumes were brilliant. In the second act, I wore one seductive red velvet gown with a matching hat perched on my curls. My real hair had grown to shoulder length, and the fall I had been wearing to extend my own hair was styled in ringlets. I used it for many years in various roles. I still can't bear to part with it, although now it just comes out for costume parties.

I enjoyed a big success as Musetta, and a lot of pleasure. Amazingly, it didn't rain at Stern Grove, and the audience had their picnics and wine and lounged on blankets on the grass while they watched us perform. When I think back to that experience of singing in front of thousands of people, what astonishes me is that I did it with such exuberance and fearlessness! That is the glory of youth.

I pictured my father sitting on a cloud, watching me perform and being proud that I was an opera singer. I didn't think about my mother. I also imagined that he urged the newspapers to pick my picture, because of the inordinate amount of publicity I received.

Papagena was a very small yet charming roll. I portrayed an old woman who is transformed into a young bird-like creature. She had one duet and a cute bird dance in a short orange tutu with matching tights. It was a nice little beginner part that was suited to my physique and voice, although not very challenging in the vocal department, mostly a lot of "pa-pa-pa" chirpy sounds. How lucky I was to nab two good parts that first summer of opera.

We did our makeup in the Paul Masson cellars, where they had originally aged their red wines. They had stopped producing in the early 1950s and used the venue at the top of the hill in Saratoga, California for concerts and operas, but the aroma of the vintages that had been aged in the cave that was the backstage facility was intoxicating. A great deal of their product was served at the reception after the opera, the beginning of my appreciation for California wines. In the '60a, they were in their infancy, as far as being known outside of the state.

In San Francisco, we had all our classes and rehearsals at the War Memorial Opera House, the home of the opera company, with the stage door diagonally across from the Haight-Ashbury district, only a five-minute walk away. This was 1968, and that infamous neighbourhood was in full swing. I spent a lot of time tripping over stoned bodies, with the acrid smell of marijuana hovering in the air. The area was cheap and convenient to classes. I found a very small and somewhat disgusting furnished apartment that fit my limited budget. All my training was paid for by my win at the Vancouver audition, but the accommodation was on my ticket.

The apartment had a devil-to-open Murphy bed, a minuscule filthy cooking space with a two burner hot plate, and tons of cockroaches, the beetle kind, that I struggled to evict. If I wasn't careful in the small bathroom, I could pull the faucet off the wall in the shower, which I did once and almost scalded myself. When I asked about garbage disposal, the landlord informed me, "Just throw it out the side window into the alley. It will disappear."

Although I didn't experiment with marijuana, a couple of singers did indulge, and they were always late for the morning classes. Gossip floated around about where they were and what they were doing. They were very happy, silly, and a bit spacey when they did make an appearance, but they managed to sing well despite this. I would have thought the smoking would be hard on their throats, but perhaps they didn't do as much as I envisioned.

At the beginning of the course, I was diligent—very disciplined and serious. Things changed after we got underway. I started to relax a bit. I went on a date with one of the other singers to a party on a houseboat moored in San Francisco Bay. The host was the producer of a new hit stage show called *Oh! Calcutta*. Pot and bare-breasted women were everywhere. We left and ended up at a movie that had just opened, called *The Odd Couple*. I laughed until my stomach ached.

I knew there was a controversial war going on in Vietnam, that a group called The Rolling Stones was popular, and that my earlier idol Elvis got married, but I somehow missed the 1960s' drug craze even though I lived in the midst of it all. There was much I was a prig about, but not so much when it came to men.

Before I left Vancouver, Robert told me that I was a bit too obsessed with him, likely because I had so little experience with other men. I was determined to change that and make him jealous. That summer, I dated two different guys, who came with recommendations from friends in Vancouver. The first was magnificent looking, although extremely skinny and a smoker. People were not as anal about smoking then as they are now, but I hated the second-hand taste and smell of tobacco. Kevin came to hear *La Boheme* at Stern Grove and take me home. He drove a Mercedes Coupe convertible, dressed as if he stepped out of a fashion magazine, and was a serious opera buff. We had some stimulating evenings together, but in bed, he just wasn't up to it, pun intended, and after much discussion, he told me he thought he was gay. Unfortunately, I hadn't yet learned that every girl needs a gay boyfriend to hang out with, so I dropped him. Silly me.

The second was a professor at Berkeley, and Irish. He had a convertible Porsche, and a compelling personality. He was sexy, intelligent, and arrogant, and wore a beard. I met his Berkeley friends, and there were many intense discussions on every topic, that ranged late into the evenings. We visited the seedier parts of the city and the Castro, a very gay area filled with transgender clubs, that were a revelation to me. He rented a motel room near the Masson vineyards, where I was performing in *The Magic Flute*, and the last evening after the final show, I agreed to stay with him. He had a lot to drink, became belligerent and angry, and beat me up. I am not sure what I said that had set him off. Maybe nothing. He threw me on the floor, slapped my face, grabbed my arms and squeezed them until they ached, kicked my thighs, and left me crying, while he collapsed on the bed and fell into a deep snoring sleep, satiated.

It was disturbing and scary. I curled up on the floor and waited until morning, as I had nowhere else to go, or so it seemed at that time. I was stunned because I had never experienced anything like that, nor had I read about physical abuse. Certainly in those days things like that were not discussed.

When he awoke, he apologized profusely and drove me back to San Francisco to my apartment. Fortunately, the opera program was over and I was shortly heading up to Vancouver, where I could nurse my wounds, mostly bruises, and I can really bruise. I dropped him and told myself that I would never date bearded, Irish professors, who teach at Berkeley and drink. That may sound a bit flippant, but I don't think I was overly affected by the incident, except that I became aware that there were men who could drink excessively, and I would avoid them. I didn't tell anyone about the incident until many years later. Putting the experience out of my mind, I concentrated on seeing Carrie and Robert again, and moving on.

On the final evening of my stay in San Francisco, there was a party for all the participants hosted by the wealthy opera donor, James Schwabacher, known to all as Jimmy. He was a major benefactor of the opera company and the Merola program. Having been a singer at one time, he was dedicated to mentoring and supporting young artists. He held an elaborate dinner party in his palatial home for all the Merola graduates and a selection of his friends. His magnificent townhouse was contemporary as well as classically elegant. The ceilings were over twelve feet in height, and there were marble floors with parquet inserts of wood. The art was hung as if it were in a gallery, and immense picture windows offered a breathtaking view over the rooftops of San Francisco towards the bay.

In the main room were set up twelve tables, each seating ten. The legs of the chairs were painted with gold leaf, while the seats were embroidered in gold and leaf-green silk. The dinner service was gilt-edged. The food was exquisite, but I was too keyed up to eat. I wore a fur dress—well, a fake fur dress, but it was unusual. It looked like a fitted coat, and was dark brown and smooth as a beaver's pelt. I had tied my hair back in a long ponytail, and I was fussed over and admired.

Moët et Chandon champagne was served in flutes. I had never seen flutes before, nor had I tasted good champagne, and I started to develop my deep appreciation for it. It is still my favourite drink. Give me a bath and a glass of bubbly, and I am a happy girl. All of this was intoxicating, but I glided through it as if it were natural for me. I had been taught good manners as a child, and they had not left me. Although I was filled with awe at the surroundings, I felt quite at ease in them. I had a chance to talk with Kurt Herbert Adler, the well-respected general director of the San Francisco Opera.

Robert had recently informed me that he was moving to Toronto to become the music officer at the Ontario Arts Council. I was torn between following Robert and becoming a student at the Opera School at the University of Toronto or going to the Metropolitan Opera Studio in New York, where I had won the opportunity to be a participant. I didn't tell Mr. Adler of my romantic involvement, but asked which program would be best for me. He highly recommended the University of Toronto for my stage of development. He knew Herman Geiger-Torel, who ran the Canadian Opera Company, and he thought I would get better training there.

I returned to Vancouver and my little girl, who had been well looked after by Elsa, the German nanny, and was completely toilet-trained at two. "Ve haf vays of making you sit on zee toilet," I imagined her saying. Carrie spent her days being spoiled by both Nanny Mac and Elsa, doting women. They cut off her long red hair, because they were sure it would then grow in thick and luxuriant, which it did. But it may well have turned out that way because I have thick and luxuriant hair.

Carrie seemed to take my absence in her stride. I started bringing her special gifts from my trips, usually a Snoopy toy or little mice for a collection. She never cried when I left, and seemed perfectly content with her situation and the love showered on her by my surrogates.

She had grown up during the time I was away. The toilet training part turned out to be a real pleasure, and she made no mistakes. We hugged and laughed at nothing in particular. She was running around everywhere. There was so much joy in her. People would ask me if it was difficult having a child and striving for a challenging career. I always replied that she kept me grounded, and she did.

Robert came over after my return. On my own in San Francisco, I had become more confident—achieving success in the Merola program and performing in two major productions to much acclaim. I had met some very sophisticated people and held my own. I had experienced other relationships, albeit not very satisfying ones, but nevertheless enough to make him jealous and more interested in me.

I applied to the Opera School, and had to travel to Toronto for the audition. I don't remember what I sang, but I had already amassed a pretty good list of arias I could sing well. I must have included "Musetta's Waltz" and some coloratura aria that showed off my high notes and flexibility. I do remember that my examiners included Mr. Torel, Anthony Besch, the new director of the opera school, and Ernesto Barbini, the music director. They immediately offered me the lead role in Rossini's *Il Turco in Italia*, the first production of the opera school's upcoming season, and a full scholarship sponsored by the Canadian Opera Women's Committee.

I had been performing in front of huge audiences in San Francisco and exuded confidence. Mme. Hendrikse had guided me through all sorts of singer's repertoire that included art songs of French, German, and English composers. She required that I learn oratorio, large-scale sacred compositions for soloists, choir, and orchestra. I was becoming a very poised singer.

Before I left Vancouver, I sang the "Monteverdi Vespers 1610", a little-known work, with the Vancouver Symphony and Vancouver Bach Choir, under Meredith Davies, one of my first professional experiences. I was proud of my natural trill, but made the mistake of telling Robert. He wrote the review of the concert and, although it was complimentary, he said at the end, "her trill was too loud." That was when I learned never to trust a critic, or a reporter, for that matter.

It was only one year since I had left Whitehorse. No wonder I impressed them at my opera school audition. I was already working as a professional when I went there. There was no doubt in my mind about my ability. I knew that my grounding was shaky, particularly in the theoretical part of music. I never could tell what key I was singing in for example. I could barely play the piano. As a child, I had learned it and passed conservatory exams, but I certainly wasn't capable of accompanying myself, and even though I played string bass in high school, it didn't prepare me for the complexities of an opera score.

As a result, I had to spend hours studying just to keep up. It hurt me when Robert criticized my singing, but I just continued to get better and trusted that he had a good ear. Some of the others had larger richer voices, that were quite glorious in timbre. Mine was light, pure, flexible, on pitch, and suited my personality. As long as I stuck with the music that suited me, I was fine. If I ventured into heavier repertoire, I was out of my zone and in trouble.

Robert and Riki

Riki Turofsky

Nanny Mac and Carrie

Da Capo—Back to the Beginning and Onward 1968–1970

I hired someone to drive my little red Fiat across Canada. I packed up my furniture, and hired a van to move the big items. Amidst tears and hugs, I promised Nanny Mac and Elsa that I would be back to Vancouver to visit and perform. I kept that promise for years, and Nanny Mac saw me sing my first major role.

It was hard to leave Vancouver but, in September 1968, I became a Torontonian once again. I found a charming small but very clean two-bedroom apartment on Montclair Avenue just off Spadina Road in an agreeable tree-filled part of Forest Hill Village. It was an area I knew well, shops within walking distance and close to the junior high school that I had attended. Best of all, it was not far from my sister's house. She was back in Toronto with her husband and Jordan and her daughter, Sari, six months younger than my Carrie. My excitement over the possibilities of my new life was growing.

I enrolled Carrie in Tiny Tots Day School, about ten minutes from our home. She was required to wear a uniform: red plaid pleated skirt, white blouse, and tam. On the wall in my Florida home, I still have an enlarged photo of her standing, lost in thought, in the playground. I cherish it.

I asked Mort's parents to send the furniture I had in storage. Most of my belongings arrived, but not the special small pieces, like my tea wagon from Mort's Aunt Jenny. They kept all my scrapbooks and high-school memorabilia. I was initially very upset by this, but then I just let it pass.

I didn't see any relatives. Aunt Ada was still alive, and my sister did the family duties there. I connected with my pal, Carol K. There were three Carols in my life—my childhood friend Carol Kirsh, my friend and babysitter in Vancouver Carol Lang, and my sister Carol. Along with my sister and Bernie, I visited with Mother and Father White, Sally and Neil.

Mort was on the West Coast, and I had to nag him for the support cheque each month. His brother, Elliot, lived in Toronto and became involved in Carrie's life, a meaningful relationship for her and him. He gave her little gifts and much love. His parents were non-communicative. Robert was in the city; the other two women he was involved with were still back in BC. Ah ha! My 'Ah ha' was short-lived, as *they* migrated east as well.

I quickly became accustomed to my new place and immersed myself in learning the role of Fiorilla for the big production at the opera school. Carrie adapted well to her school, was proud of her uniform, and loved having friends to play with. She seemed very happy in her new home, and I don't think she missed Nanny Mac or Elsa *too* much.

Bernie's large family welcomed Carrie and me, including us in Jewish holiday gatherings. Meanwhile, the Whites invited us for Christmas and Easter get-togethers and many Sunday dinners. I was craving family, and missed that special relaxed tranquility. At about ten years old, Jordy was still my darling boy. He started calling me *Tante*, the German for aunt. I have no idea why, but he continues to this day. Sari was a precocious little blond with big blue eyes.

I had to find babysitters I could trust, a good piano tuner, and time to spend with Robert. I knew that he was happy to have me in Toronto, but he kept me uncertain about the exact nature of our relationship. I dated him exclusively, and I believed he dated only me. We went to many concerts and operas, dinners, parties, and events. I met his acquaintances in the music world, as he was the new music officer of the Ontario Arts Council, and everyone in the business wanted him on their side when they would be applying for grants and favours in the future. No matter why we were invited, it was awesome to be part of the artistic power core of Toronto.

The opera school started in mid-September, and Rossini's opera *The Turk in Italy*, which I was slaving away to learn, would be in November. Along with preparing for the big production, we had classes that involved short scenes from mainstream operas like *La Boheme* and *La Traviata*. Thank-you concerts for our scholarship donors from the Canadian Opera Company were part of our duties, and we coached with conductors, and took acting, movement, makeup, and voice lessons.

I started working with a new vocal teacher, Irene Jessner, who was quite the opposite of genteel Mme. Hendrikse. An overwhelming personality, Jessner had sung at the Metropolitan Opera. She always spoke her mind and treated all her voice students like her children. She acted as if she owned the opera school, and us. The other teacher was Dr. Ernesto Vinci. The two of them encouraged rivalry among the singers. It was like a mini opera house somewhere in Germany. Mme. Jessner would talk very loudly whenever a singer of the *other* voice teacher was performing. She was quite rude, even incorrigible, but we were drawn to her. When she said, "Dat vas vonderful!" we were gratified.

Anthony Besch, the school director, was very modern, his direction straightforward. His British background, which included many seasons at Glyndebourne and the Welsh National Opera, brought a sophisticated approach to all of our productions. He was inspiring to work with, precise and clear, and obviously enjoyed teaching. I will forever remember his advice when I was emoting during an aria. I can actually see where I was standing in the rehearsal hall with him beside me. I was so immersed in the character's dilemma, that I was almost in tears and trying to sing at the same time. He told me, "Darling, if you get involved, then your audience won't. Get the emotions of the moment out at home when you are rehearsing. Know them, but don't let them interfere with your singing. The audience will get it!" He was demanding, but always supportive.

In the big opera, I was double cast with another soprano who had a beautiful creamy voice. She had been in the school for a while, and I am not sure how happy she was with my arrival, but she was always gracious, even when I received a better review. Many artists say they never read their reviews. Perhaps that is true for a small group, although I doubt it. I read them all throughout my career. I kept the good ones for excerpts for my bios and résumés, and they were extremely useful. The bad ones stung, but I recovered. I tried to find a reason for the negativity. Sometimes it was just *who* was writing, and then I understood.

Today, I read the reviews in the *New York Times*, a paper I get daily because it is has an arts section every day. The well-informed critics don't try to skewer the artists. They never write "the best singer in the opera was...", which is so lame. Critics can have an impact on the audience attendance at an opera or play. That is power, and a responsibility.

The avant-garde production values of *The Turk in Italy* were brilliant. The set was huge and impressive. One scene was on a raked, or slanted, stage with a billiard table. I don't remember how the ball stayed on the table, but the singers sang and played pool at the same time. Many opera lovers and reviewers came to see this rarely performed piece. In the lobby after the show, I met Stuart Hamilton, one of the foremost vocal coaches in the city and writing a review for *Opera* magazine in England. His assessment of my performance turned out to be very flattering. Our first meeting led to a long and rich ongoing friendship.

The MacMillan Theatre stage in the Edward Johnson Building at the University of Toronto, where we performed, had been constructed with the same dimensions as the O'Keefe Centre Stage, where the Canadian Opera Company performances took place. This was deliberate to give the company a precise rehearsal space. It was also good for us aspiring young opera singers, who would someday sing with the company. We watched the rehearsals with the big stars and experienced a sample of the real opera world. We went to classes all dressed up—high heels, makeup, and hair done. We were competitive and hungry for a career. You never knew whom you might meet, or who might hear you rehearse or perform in a class. I was certainly ready to be discovered.

During those Besch years, aside from the Rossini opera, we did the world premiere of Humphrey Searle's *Hamlet*. I played Ophelia, and Donald Rutherford, who was already singing professionally, was Hamlet. It was a difficult demanding piece of contemporary music, very good for us in terms of challenges, but also because many critics came from all over to review it. My brilliant costumes included a pale yellow lace gown with high Elizabethan collar. The mad scene was daunting, vocally and physically, and I became immersed in the famous character.

The opera was to be premiered in England at Covent Garden, and I was invited overseas as the cover/understudy for Ophelia, with Donald as Hamlet. He fell very ill in London with encephalitis. Victor Braun took his place and he too became ill. Unfortunately for me, the Ophelia was as healthy as a horse. I found an excerpt from Searle's memoirs about the opera where he said, referring to the première in Toronto, "The performances went very well, and we had an excellent Ophelia in Miss Turofsky."

Humphrey Searle and his wife, Fiona, entertained me in England. So that she could make a pie with a chocolate wafer crust, Fiona had asked me to bring boxes of Christie's chocolate wafers, which were available only in Canada. My suitcase smelled delicious, and was covered in crumbs.

Aria- song of a life

Their apartment was filled with papers, books, art, and dust. Soon after my arrival, they invited me for a lunch of scrumptious fish pie and much wine. At the table, Humphrey fell fast asleep, snoring noisily during my conversation with Fiona. At the conclusion of the performance, they escorted me to the local pub near Covent Garden, where I met all the theatre types. I felt very alive and special, being introduced as a brilliant young singer from Canada. Moreover, I was ecstatic that my name appeared in the program.

I walked all over London in high-heeled Maud Frizon shoes—red, blue, and white soft leather complete with ankle straps, very sexy and unusual. I stayed at Wendy Pollock's place in Herne Hill. She was singing in all sorts of local concerts, operettas, and pantomimes. There was always someone at the piano in her parlour, playing or singing or just gabbing. I learned the London tube system, enjoyed my time with her, and ruined my feet forever.

After my heady experience across the pond, I returned to Toronto to my little girl. It had not been a long trip, just under a week, and Carrie had stayed with the Whites, a visit she always enjoyed. My daily routine continued. After I finished class each weekday, I picked Carrie up at Tiny Tots and we went home to the apartment, played for awhile in a small park, and bought groceries, and then I practised.

At the opera school, we did several productions in which I was involved in a major way. One was the enchanting *L'Enfant et les Sortilèges* (*The Child and the Spells*) by Ravel. I practised singing my part of the Fire at home, and made quite a lot of noise with my loud high notes. Carrie was always listening while she played with her toys. In those days you didn't put kids in front of a television to occupy their time; well I didn't. After the Fire's brilliant aria, the little boy, or l'Enfant, in the opera says, "*J'ai peur!*" (I'm frightened). I was stunned when, hearing me sing the Fire part, my little daughter said, "I am afraid, Mommy." Ravel obviously knew how to write for and about children.

As well as the Fire part, I sang the role of the Princess. It was the first time that I used the trap, when I appeared for my big entrance from under the stage, in my beautiful blue fairy gown, singing as I slowly ascended. It was pretty and magical, my voice in the distance, growing closer and closer to the audience as I emerged. I was crazy about that part, and portraying princesses.

Robert had become an integral part of our lives. He came over most nights of the week, when there wasn't a concert to attend. When I could get a sitter, I would go with him. He was very fond of Carrie. He had a daughter of his own, Anna, who lived with her mother in Liverpool, England. He rarely saw her, although he supported them financially. Carrie filled a void in his life. He was very patient with her, and she worshipped him. As he was the only man whom I was dating, it was not confusing for her.

I believed I was the only one *he* was dating, but he made an announcement that he would be in New York for New Year's Eve. "You and Carrie and I can spend Christmas together with my parents." They lived in the west end of Toronto. "If you get a sitter, the two of us can go for a romantic getaway to Niagara Falls for a couple of nights. I have always wanted to be in Times Square for New Years, and that's where I'll go after the Falls."

"You'll go alone?" I asked, as my stomach started doing cartwheels. "This will be my first New Years in Toronto, and I was looking forward to spending it with you."

He smiled. "Well Linda has invited me to spend it with her there." Linda was the dancer girlfriend, who had moved from Vancouver to New York. I was amazed, but figured that I could change his mind, especially when we were away being romantic. However, I was sadly mistaken. He was determined to go to New York. I was so upset that I left my favourite terry robe in the motel room when we departed the Falls.

I was angry and hurt and naturally related all to my sister. She made a few calls, and I was set up with a very attractive doctor for New Year's Eve, and a long list of dates if I wanted them. The Jewish network was more than ready to welcome the young glamorous opera singer. I almost dismissed Robert, but he came back on New Year's Day after a terrible visit and expected me to welcome him back, which I did. This is the part that makes me insane now. *How could I? What was I thinking?* My sister was not pleased and I don't think she ever forgot how he treated me. Robert and I resumed our relationship, but it wasn't quite the same. I never fully trusted him again, and I realized that other men were attracted to me. Nevertheless, he still had a firm hold on my affections. When self-esteem is bashed, it is hard to see clearly.

By the new year of 1969, I started getting engagements outside of opera school, including my debut with the Canadian Opera Company in a non-singing role in *Die Fledermaus* at the O'Keefe Centre. As Fifi, I had one line, which I practised over and over, emphasizind different words: "Adele, what are you doing here?" That was all! I wore a pink gown and a white blond wig. The gown was décolleté, and I mused that if I wore my Wonderbra pushup under the costume and shaded my cleavage, whether anyone would even care about what I said. In the second act, I was a paramour to Prince Orlofsky, sung by the inimitable Jan Rubes. The last time I had seen Jan was in an opera performance in Whitehorse with the COC on tour, and I was a Yukon housewife in the audience. Miraculously, I was performing with him on the stage. *Mirabile dictu.*

Newly elected Prime Minister Pierre Trudeau was in the audience, and someone had cleverly rewritten Orlofsky's verses to include musings on Trudeau and Canada. It was a brilliant idea, except that after he started, Jan forgot all the new lines. When I heard the stumble, I was embarrassed for him. But then, he just stepped out of character, moved toward the audience, and said in his deep-voiced Czech accent, "Ladies and Gentlemen, we are so honoured to have our new Prime Minister here with us tonight that we have written special verses for him. I am going to start again and get them right this time."

Jan started again, and nailed it. The audience went wild. He then slipped back into the set where I was waiting and quietly asked me for one of my high-heeled pink shoes. He took a bottle of champagne, poured it into my shoe, and then drank from it. He was in full flight—a professional in action, one who went on to become a brilliant movie actor. I was enchanted—until I had to spend the rest of that act with one wet foot.

After we finished the run of *Die Fledermaus* in Toronto, the company went to Ottawa to perform it at the newly opened National Arts Centre. I was still Fifi in my pink décolleté gown; and although I had only that one line, I was on stage most of the show. I actually was noticed in a review that I had great charisma, an aura that drew people in, so they watched me onstage no matter how small my role. I was to be told about this *aura* thing many times as my career progressed. I think it is something I was born with.

One cast member in *Die Fledermaus* was the exceptional bass from Wales, Howell Glynne, who played the part of Jailer Frosch. He was a superb actor and singer, gave voice lessons at the opera school, and sang in productions with the Canadian Opera Company.

After the performance, the cast was told that we would meet His Royal Highness, Prince Philip, backstage. Our excitement was palpable until Mr. Torel declared in his German voice, "Ve vill only have zee principal singers meet the Prince, none of zee small parts are invited." I was disappointed, but then Howell Glynne informed Torel that there were no small parts in the theatre and that he would not be in attendance unless everyone in the cast was presented. I met the Prince for the first of many times during my career, and he was very gracious. I think my pushed-up bosom really made an impression; it couldn't have been my singing. He chatted with me for a long time, and I felt perfectly at ease in his presence.

I was still hopelessly obsessed with Robert. He kept me off balance, and I wanted to win him totally. We were not living together, as I had my place in Spadina Village, and his was on St. Thomas just off Bloor Street, near the well-known group of restaurants in the Windsor Arms Hotel called The Three Small Rooms. We became regulars at the trendy Wine Cellar and Le Provençal. Yorkville was hot then, and Robert's apartment in the midst of all the action, was tiny and charmingly English, with a wood-burning fireplace. His furniture was red and black, his favourite colors.

We became close to Jim Norcop, who had been the director of the Vancouver Opera when I had first auditioned and who had encouraged me to become a singer, and was now at the Arts Council as well, and Charlotte Holmes, who much later became his wife. Jan and Susan Rubes and many other *arts* types were in our circle. I met Boris Brott, the recently appointed conductor of the Hamilton Philharmonic Orchestra, at a dinner at the Norcops. Boris and I were to share a love/hate relationship for many years. We did make some pretty fine music together.

Boris was the original entrepreneur. He had more ideas about concerts, gimmicks, television shows than anyone I have ever met. He was talented and persuasive, but not a detail man, nor very disciplined in the actual studying of music, not when I knew him anyway. But in the beginning, it was absolutely fantastic working with him, as he dazzled and charmed me, along with everyone else he met. We were exactly the same age. He loved women, and he and I shared a certain attraction. Boris had a beautiful young girlfriend Janis, but married another attractive and smart woman Ardyth. Boris was touchy-feely and he was always caressing my face, which I loathed.

When I first met him at dinner, I had my long hair in braids. I was about to embark on an audition tour in Germany and was already starting to look like a German *fräulein*. The idea of doing a *Hansel and Gretel* together in Hamilton for a police concert was formed when Boris saw me and heard me describe the performances of *Hansel and Gretel* I had done in British Columbia on tour. Boris's idea was to do a shortened version, which would be televised locally. We found a Hansel and a witch, and Robert was in charge of the oven. Not a good idea, as he had that history of the singed eyelashes, but it was a very low-budget performance.

Boris spent most of the rehearsal time on the overture. With its rich orchestral texture, Humperdinck's opera demanded this attention. He worked his way through much of the music at the beginning of the opera but, as I was to learn over the years, Boris often never made it through all of the music to the end in a rehearsal. He was terrific at winging it though, and the concert was a success. He could schmooze an audience better than anyone with his talk and humour and was worshipped. That was December 1969 in Boris's first season with the Hamilton Philharmonic at the Palace Theatre. (Hamilton Place didn't open until 1973.) Members of the orchestra included what was to become the famed Canadian Brass. I was very busy performing, and I still hadn't graduated.

The Canada Council awarded me a grant for young artists, which I used to finance an audition tour of German opera houses, with the hope of landing a guest position in one of them. Before this trip, I had found a New York agent, Hans Hoffmann, who was eager to represent me and who had contacts with a German agent, which was the route I had to pursue.

I arrived in Vienna with a miserable full-blown cold and was forced to rest in bed at my budget hotel for a few days to get better. I learned to speak German with the chambermaids. I had a good ear for languages, and there was definitely a need. When I was fully recovered, I commenced my audition tour at opera houses in Stuttgart, Frankfurt, and Munich. I really hated Germany. I felt like a foreigner; well I was a foreigner. On one of the trains, I sat opposite what I imagined to be a Nazi officer in civilian clothes. I had seen so many movies about the war, and he looked the type. The train personnel wore very Nazi-like uniforms as well.

I was treated properly in all the auditions and in the German towns that I visited, but there were still so many reminders of the war less than thirty years before. I kept thinking of the Jews in Germany and the horrors they had suffered. I cut short my trip, knowing I could never be happy living and working in that country. I couldn't wait to get back to the Opera School, and Toronto.

I started and ended my audition tour in Vienna, a picturesque city with magnificent buildings and elegant boutiques. I mostly window-shopped on Sundays, when all the stores were closed, but I did purchase matching dirndls for Carrie and me at a kiosk in the train station. There, amazingly, I met up with a conductor, Dietfried Bernet, whom I had heard when he guested with the Vancouver Symphony a few years before and spent time with.

He invited me to his concert, and afterward when we went out for dinner, I consumed schnitzel à la Holstein, breaded veal with a fried egg and anchovy on top, and warm German beer. Bernet was darkly good-looking, exciting, sexy, and a bit scary. I met his colleagues from the orchestra, and was awed by his stimulating life. Google tells me he had an illustrious career, conducting in European opera houses. He died in 2011.

Before I had left Canada, I learned that the Vancouver Opera would be doing a production of Verdi's *Un Ballo in Maschera*. I had seen the opera in San Francisco the previous fall and knew that the uncast role of Oscar would be perfect for me. I let Irving Guttmann, the Vancouver Opera artistic director know that I wanted to audition.

I sang the two main arias for him and won the role. As well as seeing *The Masked Ball*, I saw Luciano Pavarotti in *La Boheme*. It was near the beginning of his career, and even then his vibrant voice resonated through the opera house. I was glad to have heard him in his first major North American performance.

It is hard to describe my elation, knowing I would be singing a major role on the stage of the Queen Elizabeth Theatre in Vancouver. It was only three years since I had started singing seriously, and I was being given a chance to prove myself. Irving Guttman was a canny director. He had an ear for casting, as well as an eye. I had some experience singing in San Francisco and Toronto, and I was obviously not going to fall apart with nerves. He took a chance on that, and on me.

Oscar, the young pageboy, is a pivotal character in the tragedy. I wore my long hair in a ponytail, tied at the neck with a black ribbon. I sent my measurements to the opera company; when I arrived for my first fitting, all the costumes were huge. Astounded, I asked what had happened. Luigi, the costume fitter responded, "All the singers send the size that they wish they were, so we make the costumes much bigger to fit them." The designer, Suzanne Mess, was pleased to costume a slim Oscar, who actually was able to look like a boy. I practised the walk and the exaggerated seventeen-century bows. I had the moves down, and the music sat easily in my voice. It was May 1970, and my official debut as a professional. My colleagues were the big guys—conductor Mario Bernardi, and Louis Quilico, who sang Renato, and other fine singers.

I met the French-Canadian bass, Claude Corbeil, and fell for him. He was very charming and, I learned later, quite the womanizer in the opera world. The flirtation added another dimension to my opera experience. Perhaps I wasn't as much in love with Robert as I thought. I was starting to become confident, and independent, and Robert *was* on the other side of Canada. Hmm....

The rehearsals went well, and I was ready for opening night. I was tingly with nerves and excitement. Before I went out on stage, I went to the restroom so many times I couldn't believe it, and I cleared my throat. I felt like some racehorse at the starting gate and kept wondering if I would remember all the music, but of course it was there for the dress rehearsals and was ingrained.

For my entrance, I marched across the stage, my buckled shoes going "tap tap tap" on the riser just above the stage, and then I stopped to sing, "*S'avansa il conte*" (The count advances) and made a flourishing bow. It was a good way to start. I could sing that simple phrase loudly and not worry about my voice shaking.

All went extremely well. On stage and prepared, I was in a heightened state of consciousness, knowing where to move, what to sing, listening to the other singers and to the orchestra, being aware of the lighting, always thinking ahead. It is a zone of clarity. This zone is comparable to that of a highly trained athlete, who has that perfect baseball pitch or tennis serve or golf drive, and then the game to follow it up. It is an exalted state of being in the moment.

I stayed at Nanny Mac's, where I knew Carrie would be looked after, so I brought her with me from Toronto. She attended an orchestral rehearsal, and I charged her with taping my part. I had a Uher reel-to-reel tape-recorder, which I taught her how to work. "Every time you see Mommy on stage, turn on the play/record button, and when I leave, turn it off." She did this very well. I explained that it was so that I could hear what I sounded like in the large theatre and that would help me with the performance. She was four years old at the time. Later, when I was listening to it, right in the middle of one of my arias, I heard this little voice whisper, "Mommy, I have to go to the bathroom!" I laughed out loud. I guess she assumed that I could hear her, too.

Carrie and I had a memorable time in Vancouver with Nanny Mac and Elsa. When I wasn't rehearsing, we walked to Kitsilano Beach, ate fish and chips wrapped in newspaper, or visited the bears at Stanley Park, one of her favourite sites. She talked incessantly about her Snoopy toy and his clothes. My sister, her Auntie Carol, came out to see the performance, and we all spent some pleasurable time together. She was very proud of me and my accomplishments. Robert did not come to see me in my major debut role, but he sent roses and a witty card.

The opera was an enormous success. I don't think it had been staged before in Vancouver—it was classic, melodic Verdi, with magnificent ensembles, arias and the right mix of tragedy and mystery. I garnered rave reviews. Max Wyman, critic for the *Vancouver Sun*, wrote such glowing comments that I used them in my press materials for years. "Her sweet, true elegant voice soared in the theatre" is one phrase I recall.

My most enduring memory of *The Masked Ball* was singing in the big ensembles. As my voice floated out into the hall, I experienced a vivid elation, knowing that I could be heard over all the other voices because of the way that Verdi structured the melodic lines. This singing in ensmbles with my vocal line above all the others is what I miss about performing.

Aside from being well rehearsed, artists do many little things that are necessary for their peace of mind, many of which become habit. Mine included drinking a glass of ginger ale to clear my throat and settle my stomach, arriving early at the theater, and making sure my special good-luck objects were set just so near the mirror—a little pink stuffed hippo that was a gift when I sang the role of Oscar, cards from well-wishers, a special pin from Suzanne Mess who was my designer on many productions, a picture that Carrie drew for me and signed "I love you, Mommy."

I would also check my costumes, and try to calm down, and do things in an exaggerated slow way. Before a show, I always had a nap and ate a good dinner—in the beginning it was meat, and later on, pasta. I vocalized enough to be confident that my high notes and low notes were present. I learned early on that I could warm up the voice too much before a show and have nothing left for the performance. In opera school, I practised some difficult high phrases for my role in Mozart's *The Impresario* so many times before I went onstage that I was barely able to sing them when it mattered. I always reviewed the score. I didn't talk too much, but was happy and friendly with everyone in the cast as well as the stagehands, stage manager, and orchestra members. I usually did my own makeup

Aria- song of a life

and hair, and often had little gifts or cards for the other performers. All of this preparation was to instill a sense of well-being and turn my nervous energy into excitement before the performance. Which it did.

Carrie's birthday, Riki and cousin Sari 1968

La Boheme at Stern Grove, credit: official publicity still Merola Opera program 1968

Accelerando— Moving along Rapidly 1970–1972

I had booked a July 5 flight for Los Angeles, but changed my mind at the last minute and rebooked for the following day. That plane I had planned to take—en route from Montreal to LA with a stop in Toronto to pick up passengers—crashed in Toronto. The pilot, Peter Hamilton, was the brother of Stuart Hamilton, my coach. I was unnerved, not only because I would have been at the airport ready to board when the crash occurred, but because Stuart's brother was killed.

Air Canada's excellent record made it even more disconcerting. There was no specific reason why I changed my flight except for a strange feeling that I had about going that day. Then, it was simply a matter of calling Air Canada—you could get through immediately, no charges for changes or penalties—and switch flights. Flying was much simpler, no security at the airport, just arrive a half hour or so before the flight, and voilà you boarded, with all your luggage checked.

I was going to California, because I had heard about a very fine program for musicians at the Music Academy of the West, Santa Barbara. The campus was housed in a huge private estate, which spanned forty-five acres and was only minutes from the Pacific Ocean. It was a postgraduate course for singers, all of whom received scholarships. I applied and was accepted.

When I called Mother White and asked if she would look after Carrie for the summer, she replied, "Of course, Carrie just loves the farm, and she'll stay in your old room."

Although Robert and I were still spending much time together, I was making my career decisions independently and knew that the program in Santa Barbara was not to be missed. I was still in love with Robert, but not as possessively. I wasn't worried about our relationship weakening while I was away. It was such a great opportunity, and he expressed a desire to visit me there.

The director of the school was Martial Singher, a famous French baritone. Lotte Lehmann, the renowned German soprano, was the master class teacher in German lieder, and the acclaimed Maurice Abravanel was the conductor of the orchestra. There were classes in every aspect of performing. I was assigned the role of Nannetta in *The Merry Wives of Windsor* on the basis of a taped audition.

In Santa Barbara, I met my classmates and started the search for a place to stay. Many residents offered their homes for rent to academy students, and I found one that appealed but was not in walking distance. One of the tenors, Michael Rosness, had a Karmann Ghia convertible and he needed money to make insurance payments. We struck a deal, and I had a very smart midnight blue convertible for the summer. My accommodation was the garage of a charming hill house. My second time living in a garage—memories of Nanny Mac's in Vancouver—only this one had a swimming pool that I could use, a hot plate for cooking, a small fridge, and a narrow bed. Outside was a lemon tree, inside thousands of tiny ants. Once the Santa Barbara fog lifted every morning and the sun rose over the mountains, it was glorious.

My scholarship paid for the tuition, and the Canada Council covered the travel arrangements. Mort was still supporting us, the $500 going a long way in the early 1970s. I put my singing earnings in the bank, never used a credit card, but lacked contingency except for about $5,000 left from my parents' estate.

Our first sessions were with M. Singher, a wiry energetic man who told it as it was. He was relentless in his appraisal of our singing. If you could take the criticism, you could achieve great things. The big surprise for me was that he and M. Abravanel, the conductor, decided that I was not a Nannetta but a Mistress Ford, when they heard my voice and saw me in person. Mistress Ford is a huge part, the star soprano in the opera. Although there was a double cast, as usual in these training programs, I had to quickly learn and memorize the role to be ready to start coaching rehearsals in less than a week and then staging rehearsals. The role was musically and temperamentally right, but I had not planned to work like I did when I arrived.

I had prepared French arts songs for M. Singher and lieder for the nerve-racking Friday master classes with Mme. Lehmann. Like a monarch on a grand old throne, she sat to the side and listened intently as we performed. She worked with me on my piece, and commented, "The song starts ven zee music starts. You should be in zee mood immediately, not just ven you zing, but from zee first notes in the piano or orchestra." Too few singers have the commitment that Mme, Lehmann demanded.

Every day, I was busy attending class, learning music, and killing ants. I started inviting other singers for dinner. It was a challenge on two hot plates, but everything was possible with a sense of humour. We drank good wine, and some very nice friendships developed. Lev, the singer who played Falstaff, was six-foot-seven, a huge man with a deep voice. The tenor Michael and I became very close, as sopranos and tenors often do. The three of us went everywhere together and became fast friends—the Three Musketeers. A mezzo called Heidi almost joined us, but she was preoccupied with some weird fad diet of eating only zucchini and she worried about her voice all the time. This proved boring for the rest of us.

Missing my baby girl, I called Carol Kirsh in Toronto and asked her to bring Carrie out for a visit. Carol worked, but I figured she needed a holiday, and I sure needed my child—her sweet smell, dimples, red hair and her delight and wonder at new experiences—everything. The airfare wasn't exorbitant, and we could all camp in the garage together.

I met them at the airport and managed to fit us all into the two-seater convertible— no seat belts then—and found a place to eat that was suitable for kids. There was a playground, where Carrie went on amusement rides and then vomited from the whirling around or her excitement. We went to my place, unpacked, and then played together in the pool.

Carrie hadn't changed much since I had last seen her; perhaps her vocabulary had increased a little. I savoured our brief time together. We didn't talk about missing each other either, and waved goodbye cheerily at the airport knowing we would be back together again in a few more weeks. I always had a lump in my throat when we parted but accepted my fate. What a good friend Carol was, and still is. If I had been in a normal marriage, I would have been at home with Carrie, but probably wouldn't have become an opera singer. I loved my career, and it was part of the job to travel, study, audition, and perform. I knew she was always in good care. I didn't *allow* myself to feel guilty.

Carrie seemed to understand why Mommy was always coming and going. I would bring her toys, like her cherished Snoopy doll, which I still have, albeit in a ratty condition. I continued collecting mice for her on every trip. I've kept them on a glass shelf in my bathroom, where I can see them every day. She looked forward to the gifts, our hugs, and companionship; I looked forward to our intimacy when I returned. The opera performances went very well, as did my master classes. I departed Santa Barbara with a wealth of knowledge, experience, and as a much better singer.

On my return to Toronto, I was full of new ambitions and joy. This euphoria was short-lived, when a truck ran a stop sign and hit my little Fiat. The front window of my car shattered filling my face with glass shards. I smashed my knee against the dashboard, an injury that has plagued me for years. I was rushed to Toronto General Hospital, where I had the presence of mind to call my brother-in-law on staff there, to get his help finding the right doctor. He did, and my face mended perfectly.

I tried to reach Robert, but couldn't find him in Ottawa, where he had gone for a meeting. When I called his hotel room, a woman answered the phone. A well-known pop/folk singer from Vancouver, whom he had known from his critic days, was staying at the same hotel.

When he returned to Toronto, he was very apologetic, but the damage was done. I felt betrayed when I learned about his tryst. Amazingly, I stuck with him. I still didn't have the confidence to be on my own. He was older, strong, and powerful, and had some magical hold over me. He was a male presence in Carrie's life and helpful when I was travelling. *Here we go again.* Another man who couldn't remain faithful to me. Damn.

Before the accident, I had been hired to sing Zerlina in *Don Giovanni* with the Canadian Opera Company in their fall season. I was double cast with Gwen Little, whom I had heard in Whitehorse eons before. I couldn't possibly imagine that I would be sharing a role with her. I had very low-cut costumes with pushed-up décolletage, par for the course for sopranos, it seemed. My costumes in *Merry Wives* were the same: slim waist, bosom displayed, full skirts, hair in ringlets cascading down my shoulders, and you have the picture. Justino Diaz was the Don—a sexy and well-sung Don he was, but he was also very professional and kept his flirting on the stage.

My sister was so delighted that I was performing in Toronto that she threw a party for me, the first of many parties over the years in her superb style. Every aspect matched the theme of the opera or occasion she chose to honour. The food, wine, flowers, décor, invitations, every single detail was perfectly coordinated. And the parties were entertaining, too. Musicians can really drink and celebrate, and I'm sure we all sang at some point at that *Don Giovanni* fête.

One week later, I flew to Vancouver to do a CBC radio concert of *Riders to the Sea*. It was broadcast live in front of an audience. I was Nora, and needed to sing with an Irish accent. The music by Ralph Vaughan Williams is hauntingly beautiful, sad, and touching. I scored a hit there too. I was well launched in my career. It was September 1970, only three years since leaving Whitehorse. It seemed a much longer time. I was twenty-six, Carrie was four, and Robert almost forty. The amazing thing was that it felt natural, as if I had been working to become an opera singer all my life.

Whitehorse was becoming a hazy memory. My marriage to Mort seemed totally unreal, except for Carrie's presence. My teen years and all the sad times weren't erased but diminished. I had moved on, and everything seemed to be following a grand plan. I was working hard, studying and performing, going to concerts with Robert, getting Carrie ready for kindergarten, entertaining, managing our finances, and keeping up with family functions. I set up the model for my future of being extremely busy and organized, and thriving on the pace. Life was good.

As far as work was concerned, I was fast becoming the flavour of the month. I sang with choirs and orchestras, and was called in at the last minute to substitute for ailing singers. One time, I learned Beethoven's *Mount of Olives* with about two days' notice. But learning a work so quickly meant that I forgot it just as quickly, whereas the opera roles that I honed over months are still with me.

The Arts Council started a new program called Contact, where performers could audition for prospective employers. I sang for the first time for the acclaimed choral conductor, Elmer Iseler. He was taking his professional choir, The Festival Singers of Canada, on tour to England and France and needed soloists. My voice was suited to the program—Handel's *Birthday Ode to Queen Anne* and Haydn's *Nelson Mass*. I was ecstatic to be hired.

The *Nelson Mass*, a challenging and very rewarding composition, featured the soprano. It was a showpiece that I reveled in. In London, we performed with the English Chamber Orchestra in St. John's Church, Smith Square; in Paris with the Radio Orchestra of France (ORTF) in l'Eglise de la Madeleine.

Ritché Couturier had provided me with some elegant gowns previously and always gave me a break on the price. They did great jewel embroidery work. I chose a chocolate-coloured chiffon that just skimmed the floor. It had a vest of embroidered gold, with flecks of pale lime green thread. The neck was high, and the sleeves were sheer, long and flared, ending in cuffs that had the same rich jeweled embroidery. I wore my very long hair (now all my own) half up, half down, and it was almost the same gold as the vest, minus the touches of green, of course. My shoes were gold as well.

After our performance in London, we attended a reception at the elegant Canadian Embassy, where we were served tiny watercress sandwiches with tea and scones. It was fussy, formal, and pleasurable. The performance went well, and the guests were friendly and complimentary. The church had an unusual exterior with two spires. The interior was austere with excellent acoustics, and the English Chamber Orchestra had made hundreds of recordings there under Neville Marriner.

Paris was definitely different. I was introduced to bidets and croissants. La Madeleine was a magnificent Roman Catholic church built as a temple for the glory of Napoleon. The audience was not allowed to applaud, so they just stood up at the end of the concert. The Canadian ambassador to France, Léo Cadieux, was a sophisticated host. The ornate embassy was splendid, and the reception incredible. I had never seen anything like the intricacies of the hors d'oeuvres; champagne flowed continually. The waiters wore white gloves. Admirers surrounded me, and the Parisian women told me how much they appreciated my gown. In those days, most soloists wore simple black sheaths and were heavier than I. The charming cultural attaché invited me out. There was as well an invitation from the head of the broadcast team for the ORTF. I was glowing and, best of all, I had sung the Mass very well.

I spent the weekend at a country inn, sampled frog legs and Dom Perignon for the first time. I bought some great boots, a perfect match for a khaki suit with a slit skirt over hot pants, that were all the rage then. On the plane, the captain invited me to ride in the cockpit most of the way back to Canada. My head, and the plane, were in the clouds.

After that tour, I began preparations for the *Tales of Hoffmann* in Edmonton. I was having one extraordinary performing experience after another. Irving Guttman chose me to be the doll, Olympia, an enchanting coloratura role.

I returned to the hotel Chateau Lacombe, where I had stayed with Mort four years earlier when I had tried to save our marriage. This time, I shared a room with Judi Forst, who was singing the part of Niklause in the opera. The two of us were quite a pair—blond, good-looking, and travelling with piles of clothes and shoes in huge suitcases. We got along famously. We were so different, but there was mutual respect. We often found ourselves dressed alike, without any discussion beforehand.

I scored a big success with Olympia, a definite show-stealer with my high notes, massive sparkly false eyelashes, and the temperament. Judi was a scintillating Niklause and won great praise. We were entertained at receptions and dinners by members of the opera board, and would diligently write thank-you notes afterwards.

By the time I returned home, it was early spring 1971. Carrie was developing quickly, and I had to decide where she should go to school after she graduated from Tiny Tots. Robert and I still lived separately but were constant companions. I saw an ad in the *Globe and Mail*—"Design your own townhouse" was the heading. A developer was renovating a group of turn-of-the-century workers' row houses in midtown Toronto and was offering them for sale. I had the down payment, and Robert had a good salary at the Arts Council, but he always lived beyond his means. If we were out for dinner, he would pick up the tab even though he didn't have the money, but he liked to be the big spender. For business, he had a generous expense account to take out clients of the Arts Council.

Robert and I shared expenses. He paid the mortgage each month—in the '70s, it was under five hundred dollars. I paid for food and small luxuries. I would save quarters in a jar until I had enough to buy specialty items, like escargots or clams or tinned lobster. He looked after utilities. I paid for all my gowns, makeup, music, hair, and coaching, but I was able to deduct these items from my income, which helped a great deal. The employers paid for my air travel for performances. I paid union fees and looked after the car expenses. He walked to work. I paid for Carrie, but I would have her support checks until she was eighteen.

I worked with the developer on the details, and we moved into 35 Bishop Street, a little dead end on the edge of Yorkville, a trendy area of the burgeoning city. Robert brought his red and black furniture, which wasn't my style, but it was the '70s, so I surrounded it with contemporary lighting. I didn't feel we could spend money on new furniture. Robert had a hefty loan at the bank, but I never owed a penny and wasn't going to start. I spent what I earned and tried to save.

In an alcove off the living room, we used bricks and boards to hold Robert's thousand or so LPs, which he had received as a music critic. Coloured acrylic cubes housed his stereo system, and a mirrored one served as an end table. The living room was a long rectangle, with the dining area at one end, complete with a red dining table set. Our main floor almost looked like a brothel. Loving the yellowness of Nanny Mac's kitchen in Vancouver and my old Wembley Road kitchen, I chose wallpaper with huge yellow daisies for my new kitchen. This sunny happy place led out to a small fenced-in gravel yard, where I could plant vegetables.

Carrie's room upstairs had red and blue geometric-patterned wallpaper. The bathroom walls had a wild animals motif. The small master bedroom was in the front, with lots of street noise, but after some time, we put an addition on the back, with one more bath. We created a much nicer space that sat like a tree house amidst the giant city foliage. Our street was in transition. Some of the old houses were renovated, and others were rundown. A Hells Angels group of bikers living across the street took to protecting me. I loved my little old house in Yorkville, even after I left it amidst great sorrow.

We became a family, something I had been craving since I returned to Toronto. And to complete the picture, we got a large black cat that we named Clara after the girl in *The Nutcracker Ballet*. Sasha, the cat at the Whites' house, had been such a good friend that I thought we should have one as well. I enrolled Carrie in Jesse Ketchum School right around the corner, and she started to make friends.

Ballet classes became part of our weekly routine. Carrie showed a real affinity for dance, as well as music. I took her to Young People's Theatre and the museum, and her cultural education expanded. She had heard more than her share of classical music. The television was upstairs and not watched a lot. Our house was filled with music and performers, and when we didn't have guests, we would listen to the stereo, read, or just discuss my career, performances, or Robert's work. Things were humming along.

Robert was a very present and active father figure for Carrie. We never heard much from Mort, who didn't write her or call, but she was naturally curious about him. His parents were not interested in seeing their only granddaughter either, although they knew we were in Toronto, and I had offered to visit them. They must have read about me in the papers, because I was always in them. I felt they never forgave me for leaving their son, even though he was the one who had been cheating. Divorce was just not a popular option in those days. I never saw them again.

Mort did not marry Peggy, and I don't know if her marriage broke up. He ultimately left Whitehorse and married a nurse called Elaine. They had two sons. I wished he had spent more time with Carrie, but he admitted he thought it would be better for her if he was out of the picture. Little did he know that children feel abandoned and that divorce is somehow their fault. His lack of interest made a big void in Carrie's life.

Mort became a surgeon. Apparently Tourette syndrome didn't affect his operating skill, though I'm not sure that I would have wanted to be under his knife. I recently saw his name on the Order of Canada list for working to make his disease better understood. Good for him.

We all spent some time with Robert's parents, who doted on Carrie, and their dog Toby, who had once been Robert's. I suggested that, since we had a house, we could invite his daughter, Anna, for the summer holidays, and I blocked out the time from my performing so I could be around. At eight, she was three years older than Carrie. We were all looking forward to her visit and to the girls playing together. I think Robert was apprehensive, because he hadn't seen her since she was a young child, and then she had been a challenging, precocious ill-trained little girl.

Anna was a pretty youngster, with the same colouring as Robert, fair smooth complexion and vivid green eyes, and long curly lashes, like the ones Robert had lost in the oven. She had freckles on her nose and thick brown curly shoulder-length hair. Her nature, however, wasn't pretty. I assumed she was jealous of Carrie, as her mother hadn't remarried and Carrie had Robert to herself. That was understandable, but she took to whisking Carrie away into dark closets upstairs and frightening her with scary stories of ghosts.

Anna was a fussy eater. She also hated going to bed, and read horror stories late into the night with a flashlight under the covers. She was very clever and manipulative, and she and Robert spent a lot of time arguing. I think much of her bravado was just that. She liked playing with Clara, although she had cut the tail off her own cat. I kept the scissors well hidden.

When we visited her grandparents for a Sunday dinner, she took Carrie outside to play in an old shed in a neighbour's yard. Anna came home alone, and we spent an hour looking for Carrie. I was very worried and frightened, and Anna seemed to enjoy our unease. The Sunters senior were upset, and Robert was furious. We found Carrie crying and upset, but knowing that we would find her. The whole incident took about an hour and a half. Robert punished Anna by smacking her bottom and speaking harshly to her. He apologized to Carrie and me. Anna was triumphant, but when it went awry, she realized that it wouldn't win her father back to her, just the opposite. Saddened by the whole visit, I again realized how difficult it is for children of divorce. We went home and never mentioned it again.

By the end of her stay, Anna was starting to calm down and fit in our little family. Nevertheless, we were glad to see her off at the airport. Strangely, she was sad to leave and shed copious tears. I think she liked the rules in the house, having a younger sister around, and, of course, being with her father. Robert didn't talk much about the visit. He *was* British after all, and emotional displays were not his thing. He had gone to Jesuit school in Liverpool, and he was definitely not a huggy feely type.

I immediately began preparing for performances at the Forum in Ontario Place, a brand new outdoor venue by Lake Ontario. The Toronto Symphony had begun a series there, and had booked Louis Quilico and me to sing in a concert version of *Rigoletto*. I was about to make my debut in Houston, Texas, as Frasquita in *Carmen*, not a starring part, but good to get myself noticed.

Carrie really liked Jesse Ketchum Public School, but I was starting to think of sending her to a private school with a more stimulating atmosphere. Robert was still at the Arts Council. I worked daily at the piano, learning music, and getting it into my voice. I spent a lot of time alone and found that I enjoyed the solitude and focus time. Those were not the days of lunches with the girls or shopping trips. Most of my performances, particularly concerts, took place on weekends. Carrie was at school all day, Robert at work, our entertaining was kept to a minimum when I was learning a new role.

For any artist, learning or working a new part is *alone* time, until they take it to their coach or singing teacher for guidance. Once I learned the music, I would rehearse with my coach, Stuart Hamilton, who would play the orchestra part, work with me on pronunciation, phrasing, expression, dynamics, and memorization.

I studied with a well-known voice teacher in New York, called Daniel Ferro. It was easy to hop on a plane and be in downtown New York within a few hours. I received a Canada Council grant to pay for the lessons. Rarely, did I stay overnight, but Robert would hold the fort if I did. I believe Robert was proud of my success, but I was not happy working in front of him, because he would criticize me and that made me very uptight.

On one of my New York trips, I auditioned for the New York City Opera and was hired on a guest contract for the upcoming fall season with the possibility of a permanent position. In the meantime, I had the Frasquita performances scheduled with the Houston Grand Opera, a return to the Edmonton Opera, some Musettas with the Canadian Opera Company, as well as many concerts.

Houston was an eye-opener. Infamous people were everywhere I went. I was invited to the River Oaks Mansion of prominent plastic surgeon Dr. John Hill and his wife, Joan. Our after-dinner entertainment in their theatre was a film of his *before* and *after* patients. He was later found guilty of murdering Joan and then was shot by her father. Another opera patron was the Count of Mauritius, who was accused of killing a Canadian in the Bahamas, Sir Harry Oakes. The wife of a prominent lawyer approached me and proposed that I bed her husband. I was stunned. These people had great wealth and supported the opera, but what a society. My head was spinning. My chest must have been whirling too, because after Houston's heat, I went to Edmonton's cold, and arrived home with pneumonia.

The trip to Houston was very successful, and I was invited back to sing a leading role in the *Daughter of the Regiment,* which I shared with the famous soprano Beverly Sills. I decided that I would just concentrate on the opera and rehearsals, and try to stay out of nefarious mansions when I returned in a few years time. Lotfi Mansouri was to be the director, and I looked forward to that collaboration.

Meanwhile, I had the engagement at the New York City Opera to think about. Aside from the excitement of singing at Lincoln Center, I had to decide if I really wanted to move to New York and accept a contract,

Aria- song of a life

but first I had to do the performances. Robert had offered to look after Carrie during the evenings while I was away. She was at school all day, and another mother delivered her back and forth to our home.

A good friend Richard Pearlman, who had moved to Toronto to take over the directorship of the Opera School, had an apartment in New York, which he offered to lend to me. I was pleased to have his place, and knew it would be loaded with books about opera, which I could peruse. I had only to pay the utilities, as it was rent-controlled and didn't cost Richard very much to keep. Situated in Greenwich Village, it was as appealing as I had imagined. The main space was filled with books on every arts topic; the kitchen and bathroom were filled with roaches. Initially, I was disgusted by the little critters, but ultimately I just gave in, and we all lived quietly together. The only thing I had to remember was that, when I returned to Toronto, I had to unpack in the bathtub to be sure that I wasn't giving my little guests a Canadian vacation. I brought only one home with me, and his holiday was very brief.

I was so enthusiastic when I started the *Carmen* rehearsals at Lincoln Center that I could hardly wait to get there every day. The part of Frasquita was not large, but the singing was important in the ensembles. I had a chance to sing high notes and wear a black wig, pretending I was Spanish. Additionally, I received a silver goblet with my name engraved on it, with the date of my debut at the New York City Opera.

Unfortunately, I found myself in the middle of an incident that completely changed my mind about moving to that city. One morning, on the way to rehearsal, I became trapped in a subway car with a person wielding a knife—the man seemed completely out of control. I tried to become invisible, and when the car came into the station, I escaped and ran all the way to the stage door of the opera house. Breathless, I couldn't sing or concentrate. The staff understood and excused me for the day.

I never again took the subway. My entire salary was eaten up by taxi fares, and a decision that had been weighing me down was made simple. I would not leave Toronto for New York. When I returned home and announced my decision to Carrie and Robert, their relief was enormous. I have never regretted that choice. Even Clara seemed more contented, but that was short lived.

Riki Turofsky

Olympia with Stage Manager Andy Hack, tenor John Alexander, director Bliss Hebert, credit: candid snapshot taken by colleague backstage

Marie in the Daughter of The Regiment, Houston with tenor William McDonald credit: backstage snapshot taken by colleague 1973

Aria- song of a life

Riki, Carrie and Tigger 1971

Minuet and Trio—The Family Gels 1972–1974

I was fully immersed in my new life as an opera singer, mother, and live-in partner with Robert. The world was askew with Watergate and terrorists attacking the Olympic Village in Munich, but my very focused career continued. At seven, Carrie was showing real talent in her ballet classes and was invited to audition for the school of the National Ballet of Canada. We were told that she had the perfect physique, which they apparently knew by measuring her feet and other parts of her body.

Carrie was becoming quite beautiful—with long straight thick red hair, blue eyes, and no freckles, which was unusual for a redhead. She enjoyed dancing, but she wasn't one of those kids who really *wanted* to be a ballet dancer. She had seen *The Nutcracker* and loved it, but the desire to study dance for many hours every day wasn't there, and I wasn't sure that would be the right track for her, as flattering as it was. Nevertheless, she continued with the weekend classes.

I enrolled Carrie in Bishop Strachan School, a highly respected private all-girls school, for which Mort agreed to pay the fees. Soon after Carrie started at the new school, Clara was trying to deliver her first litter, and having a miserable time. Carrie and I went down to the basement where she had hidden herself away, and helped her release eight adorable kittens. Neither of us quite knew what to do, but we encouraged Clara, and we helped pull out the wee kittens and place them beside their mom. She was exhausted, but started licking them, cleaning them up. This was an intimate and touching moment for both of us. We giggled as the tears ran down our cheeks.

We had made the hard decision to sell them or give them to the veterinarian. After the last one was gone, Clara walked into the street and was hit by a passing car. We were devastated, and I wondered about the bad luck that went with black cats. Alas, I remembered and understood my mother's sadness at the loss of her canary. I had not given up on having a pet, so I called our friend, the conductor Elmer Iseler, who had farm-raised cats. We chose a tiny Maine Coon cat—well tiny at the beginning, with orange and grey stripes and a raccoon tail. Carrie called her Tigger after one of her favourite *Winnie The Pooh* characters. This Tigger grew enormous and took over our lives.

My celebrity was rising, and Robert was still keeping me off balance. When I travelled, I flirted with conductors and other singers, my way of maintaining my confidence as a woman. It seemed to work on a certain level, but I craved more. Robert and I still had a healthy sex life, but I desired a complete relationship with total trust. In the fall of 1974, we were sitting at our red dining table after dinner. Carrie was in bed. My cooking had really progressed, and we were eating tasty food and drinking excellent wine. Robert suggested we get married, or maybe I did. We set a January date. We were both feeling romantic, and it seemed like the next logical step in our relationship. I knew I couldn't trust him, and perhaps I couldn't trust myself, but I just came to the conclusion that most men will cheat when offered the opportunity. It was the era of free love.

We decided to not have children together, and I had my tubes tied. Sorry now that I didn't have any more children, the timing would have been wrong for my career, and I am not sure it would have been great for Carrie, who was eight; I was thirty, and Robert forty-three, and she was the centre of our world. We married at City Hall and celebrated with a small reception for our friends and a few relatives at our Bishop Street house. I wore a green long dress, and Carrie wore black with a white apron front. The deed was done. Nothing much changed after the marriage. We still sat in the living room most nights on the red faux-leather chairs; listened to music, talked about my performances, our ambitions, other artists, and Carrie.

We entertained often, and I experimented with many dishes. I disliked following a recipe, and took ideas from many cookbooks and created as I went along: Most things worked out fine. One meal in particular that I cooked for Lord and Lady Harewood when they visited Toronto was unforgettable. Robert had brought Lord Harewood over to Canada to report on the state of opera in our country. He had written the definitive *Kobbé's Complete Opera Book* and was the Chair of the English National

Opera Company. Robert was fascinated with the idea of accompanying him across the country. Lord Harewood insisted that his wife be with him. The Arts Council picked up the bill, and they stayed at the elegant Windsor Arms Hotel in Toronto.

Harewood was divorced, and snubbed briefly by the Queen because of this. How times have changed in that department. In Canada, he was a big shot. He and his second wife, Bambi, the sister of acclaimed French horn player Barry Tuckwell, spent most of their time eating—massive breakfasts, two-hour lunches, English tea, and then dinner. They gave new meaning to the expression freeloaders. Both in their late forties or early fifties, they were imposingly attractive. He wore three-piece *serious* suits and was developing a paunch. She was a brunette with creamy pale skin and a certain style. Their accents were plummy. I foolishly invited them to eat at our house before we all went off to an opera at the O'Keefe Centre.

The evening began poorly, when Lady Harewood arrived wearing the same outfit as I. It was all black—which I rarely wore, the skirt mid-calf and the top high-necked. Our necklaces were different, but it was a mirror image. Mine was off-the-rack as I couldn't afford designer. I wasn't sure about hers.

We all sat squished into our tiny dining room. For the first course, I had poached whole artichokes for a long time in white wine and chicken broth. I still do this dish, and the artichokes are tender and succulent. She made a point of mentioning that artichokes should never be served with white wine, although I had cooked them in it. I had raced out earlier in the day to buy demitasses for the coffee to have a complete set. These black Wedgewood cups were sitting on our buffet, near a candelabra with dripping candles. When I started to pour the coffee, I saw wax in a few of the cups and deliberately gave those to the Harewoods. They had drunk so much all evening they didn't notice.

Soon after they left I was hired to do an operetta at the Milwaukee Operetta Festival at the Skylight Theater. The unusual piece *The Great Waltz* was a mishmash of music by Johann Strauss—senior and junior. I had no experience with Viennese operetta, except my one-line speaking part in *Die Fledermaus* at the beginning of my career, so the Viennese style of singing was new to me. I was paired with a consummate older artist from Sweden, who was a star in Milwaukee, Cläes Jacobsen. A master of that particular style of music, he was tall, handsome and debonair, and really knew his way around a stage. When Cläes arrived for his first entrance during the performance, the audience burst into a wild ovation; they idolized him. He taught me about Viennese style.

The director, Zachary Solov, was a choreographer from the Metropolitan Opera, and regularly staged dance routines at Radio City Music Hall for the Rockettes. The producer, Clair Richardson, a jaunty individual who wore a velvet French painter's outfit and smoked a cigar, did everything brilliantly on a limited budget. He travelled to Poland, where he bought inexpensive red leather boots for the dancers, and went to every bridal salon in Milwaukee to borrow gowns for the chorus. The theatre was set up so that the orchestra could ascend out of the pit on its risers and travel by pulleys to the back of the stage, a spectacular effect as long as nothing went wrong. It worked smoothly most performances; when it didn't, the stagehands had to manually operate the machinery, which was challenging and slow. There were huge chandeliers in breathtaking ballroom scenes. I learned how to waltz with my back arched away from Cläes and to phrase the music with special flare.

My Milwaukee home was a furnished apartment hotel, with a big steak restaurant called Sally's on the first floor. It had been the scene of a Mafia gang killing just before I arrived in Milwaukee, and was closed while they cleaned the blood off the furniture. This definitely added to my fascination with the notoriety of the area.

I ate smoked meats and drank beer in copious amounts. Fortunately, I could eat all I liked and not gain a pound. When I performed, I would normally lose three to five pounds a show. I still don't have a weight problem, but do watch what I eat now that I am no longer performing. However, when I get anxious about anything like a presentation or a big trip or a party that I am hosting, I lose weight.

Milwaukee was the beginning of my special affinity for operettas and, over my career, I did many Viennese concerts with symphony orchestras, working with masters of the genre like Franz Allers and Erich Kunzel. I made a good living out of the music, and I was hired for so many of these concerts that one critic dubbed me the Operetta Queen of Lake Ontario.

I had my own gowns of the era, and bought orchestral parts for the music, so that it would be appealing for orchestras to hire me. I sent this music along to the conductors ahead of time, with my specific markings for phrasing in the score. They were grateful, because they didn't have to rent the music, and I didn't charge them for the use of it. Along with the parts, I came with dialogue—little stories I would tell about the individual songs.

The audiences delighted in this light pop concert music. I did New Year's Eve concerts all over Canada, as well as the United States. At one unforgettable concert in London, Ontario, I was singing in a hall that had the dressing room above the stage, with a dark curtain over a window. When the lights were on in the room, it was possible for the audience to see me in all my glory through the curtain. I was a hit before I even started to sing. When I found out, I laughed so hard that I almost couldn't sing.

It was also a time when I was a regular feature at the Forum in Ontario Place, an amusement park on Lake Ontario in Toronto, where many concerts were presented. I sang with the Toronto Symphony, the Mendelssohn Choir, and the Canadian Opera Company, and I was the classical artist in the variety shows offered by the management. I enjoyed being part of concerts with a magician, a rock group, jazz artists, or country singers. I would come out in one of my glamorous gowns, sing some showy operatic piece with high notes that usually brought the house down, and make an excellent fee. This type of mixed performance, highlighting my talent and appearance, enhanced my audience base and helped make me popular with those who didn't know or care much about opera.

I sang for quite a few years at the Forum, and I derived great pleasure working there. The permanent seating had a capacity of three thousand, but many people chose to sit on the grassy knolls and picnic during the shows. One concert was remarkable because the automatic sprinkler system went on, soaking a good portion of the audience sitting on the hillside. Another time, I was singing an oratorio conducted by the renowned artist Robert Shaw, when a pigeon pooped on Shaw's forehead. He didn't even flinch.

Children would cry, F16 jets from the summer exhibition air shows would scream by, boats in the harbour would honk, and we would all blithely continue our performances, which were a great success even in the rain or chilly windy weather that blew in off the lake. Fortunately, the performers had some cover under the large Forum roof, even though it was open on the sides, but we were often a little damp.

The man who hired all of us was sophisticated, charming, good-looking, and a con artist. I only found this out when the doorbell rang at 35 Bishop, and I was face to face with a member of the Royal Canadian Mounted Police. My stomach lurched when he told me that he had viewed my bank account records and taken note of the amounts I was paid by Ontario Place. Apparently, the executive director, Len Casey, had paid the performers one amount, claimed to have paid us much more, and kept the difference. Len went to prison.

What amazed me about the incident was that my accounts were open to the RCMP without prior notification. When Len came out of prison for a Christmas break, I saw him at a party. He was charming, suave, and totally convincing that he had not acted inappropriately or illegally. He almost persuaded me that the performances justified whatever means he had used.

In jail, he started a business selling ladies' workout gear by Leonardo; he became the chef in the prison kitchen; and very likely charmed many of the inmates. I was happy with my fees because I was able to buy a mink coat with what I received for one concert, and no one was throwing eggs at fur coats in those days.

Carrie was excelling at Bishop Strachan School, Robert was pleased with his job, and I was making very good money from my concerts and operas, especially the concerts, because my expenses were lower—no long stays in hotels for rehearsals of three weeks or more, with many performances only a highway drive from home. As a family, we took some winter trips to Florida. We went to Fort Myers Beach and Sanibel Island, and Carrie learned how to dive, spending hours in the small pool, at our resort condominium. We walked the beaches, ate crab, tanned, and had a fine break from the cold Toronto weather. One visit there, Carrie and I managed to polish off a Sara Lee cheesecake at one sitting, and share a hearty laugh about it.

Robert began telling me about his dalliances. I remember very clearly sitting on a couch in the Florida condo, which was on the beach at Fort Myers and called Lahaina, Hawaiian for restless. The lanai was open to the sound of the sea, and the wonderful, warm Florida smells of hibiscus, and sand. It had been a lazy day, followed by a humid evening with much wine, and Carrie was in bed. In 1975, she was almost nine years old. I was thirty-one, and Robert forty-four.

We were chatting idly and then he dropped the "I spent an evening with..." on me, and I listened fascinated. I think he was trying to titillate me or make me jealous and keep me in my place, wherever that was. I was not as upset as I should have been and actually thought about doing the same myself to get back at him. I knew two of the women involved and was extremely surprised as they were my colleagues. Whew! This actually hurt me more than Robert's betrayal, but I was good at not thinking about things that didn't please me. He went through female artists at a great rate it seemed.

I thought about some of my flirtations while out of town and how close I could get to another performer with whom I worked daily for three to six weeks. Perhaps I could do what he was doing when the opportunity presented itself and not feel guilty. It wasn't the way a marriage was supposed to be, but it was the way that ours turned out. Somewhere in the back of my mind, I wished for a marriage that was monogamous, with a husband I loved, cherished, and trusted. Many years later, I got just that, but I am getting ahead of myself.

I was travelling a great deal and, when Robert wasn't looking after Carrie, she went to the Whites'. Sometimes, she had overnights at friends' or my sister's. Carrie was accustomed to my absences. When I could, I took her with me, but as she became older, it was more important for her to be in school than hanging around rehearsal rooms and hotels.

She knew I was a celebrity, but I don't think that troubled her. It may have even made her proud. She was popular in school, and I was home a good portion of the time when I was learning a new project. I was always there for her birthdays and school activities, including meeting her teachers, and we had school holidays together.

My marriage had morphed into something disparate. Robert and I still had a lot in common—a love of music, theater, and dance. I hosted dinners for him and his associates and spent time with his parents, and we had game nights with good friends playing *Trivial Pursuit*. We both took up tennis and played together, though that was not a particularly happy pairing. Ours was not a monagamous partnership. We both we were having affairs, although we never discussed them again after that night in Florida, and we still had sex with each other.. Go figure.

Aria- song of a life

Riki and Judith Forst after Duet Recital 1974

New Year's Viennese concert with director Richard Ouzounian 1974

Allegretto—Time Passing Quickly 1974–1981

I sang two operas in Kansas City, *La Boheme* and *The Marriage of Figaro*. After the performances, the conductor, Michael Charry, asked me to audition for the head of the Netherlands Opera, which was mounting a production that would suit me perfectly. Carlisle Floyd had written an opera after the Steinbeck story *Of Mice and Men*, which was scheduled as part of the Holland Festival's salute to the United States Bicentennial in 1976. Although mostly an American cast with some Dutch singers, Michael felt I would be a worthy addition, albeit Canadian, as Curley's Wife, exactly like the character in the original Steinbeck novel only better because in opera, she had arias to sing, not just lines of dialogue. She had impact. I leapt at the chance, studied some of the music, and won the part. I learned a few Dutch phrases, found an apartment in the sixteenth-century house of Cora Canne-Meijer, a well-respected mezzo soprano, and left for a June sojourn in the Netherlands.

My first challenge was getting my enormous suitcases into the apartment. They had to be hoisted by a hook outside the building up to my rooms on the top floor. I was living in a music room with a baby grand piano. There was a minuscule kitchen and an even smaller bathroom. The view was terrific, if you liked rooftops. The old house was situated beside one of the many canals and, except for the large rats that exited the water on an occasional very humid warm night, I felt safe. I looked Dutch and was constantly being asked for directions when I walked from Cora's to the opera house. When people learned I was a Canadian, they toasted and treated me very well, because of strong memories of World War II and the liberation.

The opera was intense, as were rehearsals. In the story, I was murdered and swung around like a rag doll, while singing difficult music. I became too involved in this scene, and found myself choking on the straw in the barn. I also had to lie dead-still on the stage, for what seemed liked hours, but was only minutes.

The set and costume designer, Lewis Brown, had copied all my outfits from a Sears catalogue of the 1930s, right down to springalators, backless high-heeled shoes. Newspapers lined the walls. There was even an old-looking canine, who played the role of the mangy dog, and puppies too. I wore my hair yellow blond like a '30s movie star and masses of makeup, because Curley's Wife was fascinated with Hollywood and dreamt of escaping there. I studied the play very carefully, so I could get inside the character—a needy sexy love-starved unhappy female. It was the first time I would portray a twentieth-century woman.

On opening night, I received so many roses that they had to be kept in my bathtub—you got your money's worth of flowers in Holland—and my apartment smelled like a funeral parlour. Robert didn't fly over to see the performance because he had just been hired as head of Radio Music for the CBC. Carrie wrote to tell me that he had bought some very important suits for the new job. My sister and Bernie did come, and we had a marvellous time, sightseeing on the canals and sailing on the North Sea with Michael, the conductor of the orchestra.

I relished eating the *neue* herring on the street corners and visiting the Rijksmuseum, the museum of art in the Netherlands, with some of the finest and best known paintings in the world, not only the Dutch masters. We performed in Amsterdam as well as Rotterdam, The Hague, and Utrecht. I enjoyed a stunning ovation during curtain calls and garnered excellent reviews. I realized then that I could hold my own internationally.

I wasn't the same person when I returned to Canada. I was very confident and excited about my career, when an invitation arrived to be a guest on a late-night television show *90 Minutes Live* with Peter Gzowski. It was my first time on TV, and it changed my attitude to that medium and its power. All of a sudden people other than opera lovers knew who I was.

Liking my new celebrity status, I thought about increasing it. This may not seem such a bad thing, but when you are an opera singer, you really need to focus all of your energy in that direction. On television, I sang folk songs and easy-listening favourites. I still wanted to be the opera star, but I liked crossing over, a new concept then.

I engaged an agent, who represented me in this area, and I was invited to be a guest on many TV shows. One about psychics, *Beyond Reason*, featured celebrities, and I met the pool shark Minnesota Fats, the race-car driver Sterling Moss, and David Clayton Thomas of Blood Sweat and Tears. I pretended I was a country star on *Thrill of a Lifetime*, and hosted a daily summer talk show for the *The Bob McLean* show. I even shared my recipes and sang on Bruno Gerussi's *Celebrity Cooks*.

I became comfortable on talk shows and variety shows. Walking along Bloor Street one day, I was stopped by a striking woman with a big smile. "Aren't you Ricki Turofsky?" I recognized her immediately, as she was larger than life. It was Our Pet Juliette who sang after the hockey games in the '50s and '60s and more recently had a talk show *Juliette and Friends*. She was the biggest Canadian star in television at one time, and her name was still well known.

She told me she was hosting a CBC television special and would love to have me as a guest. I think she formed the idea at the moment she met me, but I am not certain. I could sing an opera aria and do a medley of songs with her. Smiling broadly to myself, I accepted and soon started preparations with her conductor/arranger, Jimmy Dale, a charismatic appealing musician, who collected old cars. We worked at his beautifully decorated home in Rosedale; the round dining-room table always set with great detail as if guests were about to sit down and have a meal. I learned a great deal from Jimmy. He was different from the classical musicians I knew—flexible and able to improvise.

The special was taped in Vancouver, and the cast stayed at the picturesque Bayshore Inn on Coal Harbour with views toward Stanley Park. It was marvellous to be back in my favourite city. The leading man, soap star Beau Kayser, was having a sizzling romance with the designer, Czilla, who was almost old enough to be his mother; amazingly they *did* marry. The electricity of their flirtation added to the mood of the entire production and to my heady experience.

The big duet with Juliette was a clever mélange of songs, like *Yesterdays*, the old pop standard, and *Yesterday*, the Beatles tune. We wore similar filmy chiffon gowns—she in black, me in white. I sang an aria from *The Barber of Seville*, complete with set and costume, and did a sketch as a private eye with a trench coat and fedora. The rehearsals went smoothly until Robert came to visit. He found fault with just about everything and was excessively possessive of my time. I missed out on the camaraderie of the group that one develops in these situations. I resented his presence. Although the show was a success, my marriage was eroding.

When I returned home, I was asked to serve as a judge on the DuMaurier Search for Stars, a forerunner of today's popular television talent searches. I travelled from coast to coast with a wonderful group of Canadian celebrities, including Juliette. It was great fun—we went everywhere first class, ate and drank extremely well, and heard a myriad of talent. All this culminated in a television show on CBC for the winners. I even got a chance to produce the opera numbers. One of our stars was tenor Richard Margison, who has had a stellar career, but we didn't agree on Ben Heppner, who later became one of the great tenors of the world.

Carrie had seen me on TV, and took that in her stride. Her school, BSS, didn't seem impressed by my celebrity either. They were accustomed to having parents in all sorts of careers; politicos, the powerful, the wealthy, and the like. She was eleven at this time, had stopped ballet, but continued doing jazz dance with a talented teacher, Judy Jordan, at the downtown Jewish Y. After a recital performance, Carrie won a book with an inscription from Judy who called her the one "with most potential". I still have this special book. Carrie had an affinity for jazz dancing, and loved going to classes, which she did for two years, along with her cousin Sari.

An inspiring teacher, Judy became somewhat like a big sister to Carrie. I was delighted with this mentor relationship. Then, in November 1978, after returning from teaching, Judy was killed in a hit-and-run near her home. Although she was screaming under the vehicle, the driver didn't hear her because he was drunk, and she was dragged to her death. We were all shocked. It was the first time that Carrie experienced the death of someone whom she loved.

We went to the funeral, and it was a sad tragic day, complete with newspaper reporters because of the ongoing investigation into the killing. I believe that incident and its unfairness affected Carrie for a long time, for years in fact. She was haunted by the injustice of it all. The media kept it in our eyes and ears, and it was a topic of conversation and horror everywhere we went.

Meanwhile, I was invited back to Holland to repeat my performance of Curley's Wife in *Of Mice and Men* and to record with the Netherlands Radio orchestra. I then sang Gilda in *Rigoletto* in Vancouver. It was my favourite role, one that I could sing in my sleep, but I got off track with it. The famous conductor Richard Bonynge hired me, and I was euphoric to be performing a role I was born to sing. And yet, as if in some sort of nightmare, I sang it with half my voice. The director, whose name I have forgotten, had insisted that I be in the character completely as the young girl Gilda. I tried to sing it as if I were fifteen at the premiere performance, almost with a boy soprano sound. It was a disaster! I could have sung it with my full voice and still sounded young and fresh. I was impressionable and wanted to please that director so much that I totally lost sight of reality. I still didn't have the maturity and confidence as an artist to just sing it the way I was trained. Directors could be mesmerizing and demanding, and I trusted that one. What a mistake! I was always trying to please.

Regrettably, no one said anything to me at the dress rehearsal. Robert was in Toronto, or he would certainly have told me. I now understand why Judi Forst's husband always travelled to her dress rehearsals. He would be her ears and eyes. Sometimes you needed those *ears,* just to be sure you could be heard over the orchestra.

The reviews said it all. I knew the reviewer Max Wyman, who was as disappointed in my performance as I was. He later interviewed me to find out what went wrong. The following performances were great, as I sang full out, but the damage had been done. The only positive thing was that my Whitehorse friends travelled to Vancouver to hear me, and they were at one of those later performances.

I was furious with myself. Gilda was the first role I had ever studied, and I had sung the complete part with orchestra many times. I let it slip away. I had been back to Toronto during rehearsals for a television appearance and missed my flight to Vancouver because of the fall time change. I was distracted. Too distracted. My priorities were wrong. Oh, to be able to rewind!

Back in Toronto, I started preparing for a concert with the Toronto Symphony of Carl Orff's *Carmina Burana*. This helped take my mind off the *Rigoletto* fiasco. I sang the difficult soprano part with ease and pleasure, and was hired by many orchestras to sing it with them. Fortunately, the Vancouver Symphony was one of them, so I could try to erase the damage I had done. Another was at Hamilton Place, during a large conference of arts organizations.

It is a fantastic work—strong, powerful and rhythmic. After all the forte music of the chorus and orchestra, the soprano part is like a fine thread of silk. One critic, John Fraser, wrote a full-page piece about how I affected him with the aria "In Trutina." This led to a cover story in Canada's national magazine, *Maclean's*, and I became known as Canada's Sexy Soprano, thanks to the cutline under my picture. More celebrity. I didn't know I was going to be on the cover. I was on a flight and was handed a copy of the magazine, and found my face staring at me.

Carrie continued to be a good student at Bishop Strachan, and was slated to leave junior school and go into middle school for grade 7. She won a prize for "most promise" in her class, but she was getting restless. Perhaps the hormones were starting to act up. She was twelve, and she was in an all-girls school, although from time to time the girls would share activities like plays and concerts with Upper Canada College, an all-boys school.

She convinced me to send her to the Toronto French School, where her cousins had been. I thought it a good idea, especially if she ever wanted to work in Ottawa or Quebec or any national company. I was fairly fluent in French and had a strong affinity for Italian and German, and hoped this would be the same for her. She was enrolled at TFS, but it was a challenge—much catching up to do in the language, and it was co-educational, which proved to be very distracting after a girls-only school. Many of her new friends were more sophisticated than she was. The teenage years were upon us.

On a co-ed class ski trip in her second year, Carrie and some other girls in the group were found in the boys' bedrooms. They were sent home. We had an argument about this, and her newly acquired smoking habit. She was furious as only a thirteen year old could be, packed a bag, and left home by taxi—which gave a whole new meaning to run away from home—and stayed overnight at a friend's. By the next day, both of us had calmed down, and we laughed about the taxi part of her escape from home.

Carrie found a new best buddy at school, Shelley Boylen, a petite vivacious charming girl. They remained close for many years, and I am still friends with her. Carrie had a boyfriend, Owen, who took her to the school prom, her first formal. We shopped at a retro store on Queen Street for her fancy dress—black lace over pink, knee length with a full skirt. We took pictures of her and Owen, as did his parents. His mother shared my birthday, and looked a lot like me. Owen and Carrie found this quite amusing. We talked about sex and the pill, and she went to our doctor who put her on it, just in case. I think she was fourteen.

She was starting to develop a real eye for fashion and design, with funky overtones. She loved clothes, looked good in them, and enjoyed sketching outfits. I enrolled her in art classes in which she excelled. Her figure had developed, and she was perfectly proportioned. They had been right at the ballet school. She was admired wherever we went, and strangers touched her hair, which she abhorred. She wore it long, and it was still thick shiny and a deep rich red colour. Once she experimented with a soft perm and tinted the ends some strange pink colour, but that didn't last, thank goodness. When I protested she replied, "It's my hair and I can do what I like." The only response that I could muster was, "Well, I have to look at it, and it's awful."

I was doing mostly concert work and television, and spent additional time at home with Carrie. She loved music, but not my kind. She knew every rock group and collected recordings. She had taken piano lessons when she was very young, but longed for the electric bass. I bought her one, and you could feel the house reverberating, when she practised in her upstairs bedroom. She hung out with other kids who were into music and fell for a boy who played bass and piano.

Washington was black, older than she, and very hip. I liked him. Robert was not so sure, so it was decided I would take her to New York, just mother and daughter, and wow her with the city to take her mind off her new boyfriend.

Although it didn't do much to change her mind about Washington, the weekend cemented our mother-daughter bond. In New York, we stayed at the Plaza and had breakfast in bed. We wandered around Central Park. We went to boutiques in Soho. I rented a limousine to wait for us while we shopped at Bloomingdales and FAO Schwartz. Even though she was fifteen, she still loved her Snoopy doll and bought him some more clothes. At Macy's we tried on dresses and shoes and bought a few trinkets.

While our driver waited patiently for us, we visited other landmark stores. But we mostly just looked at the people on the streets—individuals with attitude, a show in themselves. We ate at trendy restaurants and read the *Sunday Times*. We reminisced. We saw a Broadway show *Your Arms Too Short to Box with God*. We laughed and hugged and teased each other. It was a truly fine weekend.

Aria- song of a life

Cover of national magazine Riki Turofsky: Canada's Sexy Soprano, photo credit Ken Bell

Susanna in The Marriage of Figaro, Kansas City Lyric, photo credit: Kansas City Lyric official publicity still 1975

Carrie almost a young woman 1976

Curley's Wife, Holland with William Neill, photo credit:
Official publicity still 1976, Netherlands opera

Rubato—Changes 1981–1984

My little Kawai piano was constantly in use. Washington, Carrie's boyfriend, spent a lot of time writing music and playing on it, and I was practising at least a few hours every day, learning a brilliant piece by Glière for a concert in Victoria. There were no words, just a considerable number of notes, high and low, and many coloratura passages. As well, I was preparing some showy opera arias, as the CBC was going to record the concert. The Victoria Orchestra would be touring around the island with me as soloist. I was greatly anticipating the whole adventure. I wasn't so sure, though, about leaving Carrie at fifteen, with her new boyfriend hanging around. I would be gone for ten days. But Robert was in charge. Carrie promised me she would behave, whatever that meant.

After the Victoria trip, I started spelling my name as it is spelled today—Riki. A numerologist had approached me after one of the concerts and suggested that I change it from Ricki. She said it would be lucky for me, as well as feminine and unique. Ironically, on a recent visit to Israel, I found it a very common name as a short form for Rebecca or Rivka. There were Riki's everywhere, even on signs.

Carrie was growing very curious about her father. She was close to Robert, and he was an excellent surrogate, but she wanted to know about the doctor who had lived in the Yukon. She had only a vague recollection of meeting him, and hardly ever heard from him. Perhaps he was waiting for her to grow up. I contacted him and arranged for her to visit out West to see where she was born. Mort had moved from Whitehorse to northern British Columbia, but he owned his own plane, so they would fly to her birthplace together.

He had two young boys, cute and rambunctious according to Carrie. I wasn't privy to all the details, but I think she was disappointed in Mort's lack of warmth and affection, though apparently he did try to relate by telling her about Whitehorse and her history there. His wife, Elaine, was cool and very protective of her children and their relationship with Mort. Carrie wasn't made to feel part of that family. In Whitehorse, Carrie and Mort visited some of our old friends and saw the hospital where she was born. She called me, as promised, and sounded anxious to come home.

Mort never sent a gift or even a card for her birthday or for any occasion, but his brother, Elliot, doted on his niece, and she idolized him. One spring break in 1982, he invited Carrie and her close girlfriends to use his condo in Florida. He rented a convertible for them to drive, as people under the age of twenty-one couldn't rent a car. Carrie was sixteen, and she and her friends were already driving in Toronto. I trusted that they would be careful.

Elliot gave unique gifts to Carrie, and he never forgot her birthday. It was hard to believe that the two brothers were brought up in the same environment. Elliot took Carrie to concerts. He was a fan of Dionne Warwick and, although this wasn't Carrie's kind of music, she liked going with him. He helped her get some summer work at a photo store, where his girlfriend, Sandy, was employed. He was very present in her life and always available. She had a torn photograph of Mort wearing a parka, obviously taken up north, which she kept pinned on her cork board in her bedroom. She obviously missed him on some level.

After her trip up north, I was standing in my kitchen trying to defrost some frozen smelts for Tigger's dinner when the phone rang. Someone from the CBC asked if I would be the English-language host for the Royal Constitutional Gala in Ottawa to take place in April at the National Arts Centre in the presence of the Queen and Prince Philip. Prime Minister Trudeau would be there, as would every important person in the government. It would be telecast nationally, and would be followed by a reception and dinner with their Royal Highnesses.

What an invitation! Of course, I had already hosted quite a few shows for the CBC, was featured in a musical comedy special, and appeared on numerous other broadcasts, but this one would be watched by thousands, and would be a mix of ballet, opera, pop, and folk. A male French-language host would partner with me.

The only problem was that I had a previous engagement to perform a Viennese concert in the brand-new Centre in the Square in Kitchener, and it was sold out. I called the conductor, Brian Jackson, who happened to be British, and anxiously asked him what he suggested. He said, "Riki, you absolutely must do the Royal gig. If you can hire a plane to fly you here, then I will hold your selections until the second half of the concert after the intermission."

The Gala was scheduled for six-thirty in Ottawa. I booked a limousine to meet me at the stage door to take me to the airport where a private jet was waiting to fly me to Kitchener at nine o'clock after the reception. I had my gowns for the symphony concert; I usually changed at intermission into a second outfit. I would be performing the next night as well, so I would need those. For the first Kitchener concert, I would wear only the one, a distinctive champagne-coloured chiffon period gown with a pleated and embroidered frill around my shoulders and on the hem. It had about thirty tiny silk buttons, and it skimmed the floor. I had found it in Amsterdam.

I chose an Elizabethan green-velvet jeweled gown for the Gala in honour of the Queen. This had bell sleeves lined in gold that were very dramatic. It was the gown I wore on the cover of *Maclean's*. The only problem was that the zipper had broken as I was dressing, and one of the costume assistants had to sew me into it. I decided not to worry about that until later.

The television show went well. At the formal reception, I was presented to the Queen and Prince Philip. I had practised my curtsy and had it down. The Queen was tiny and very gracious, and had creamy smooth skin. I loomed over her. The Prince was as flirtatious as always. He even suggested that I might like to join him in California, but I was on my way to the concert in Kitchener and politely said so, and no. Amusingly, I noticed that the Queen was watching her husband very closely while he talked to me. He did have a reputation as quite a roué.

The host, Prime Minister Pierre Trudeau, admired and venerated female performers who were bright and good-looking. I had once attended a formal dinner of his as an honoured guest, and the entire head table was filled with women. The first time I met him personally was at a *Juno* awards show. Although he was not a tall man, he was imposing. He smiled a lot, was very complimentary, extremely charming, and very sexy. Power is sexy. I was captivated. He had taken to calling me from time to time, and invited me to meet his sons at a ski resort in Banff. He was separated from Margaret, but I was still married. I would have loved to get to know him better. However, it was too public an arena for a married woman, and

I declined. I cherish a letter he sent, with a picture of him with his sons, and in it he described how special I was. It is framed and hanging with many of my performing pictures in my downstairs guest bathroom, just off the living room in my Toronto home.

The reception was splendid, but I couldn't enjoy it fully because I was watching the clock, knowing I had to leave. The limo was waiting, and I was still in my gown, which I couldn't get out of. It started to rain when we arrived at the airport, where the plane was preparing for takeoff—quite thrilling to have a pilot all to myself. Although there was champagne, I couldn't drink because of my impending performance. The rain turned into a major summer storm with lightning and thunder, but fortunately it was a short flight.

A member of the board of the Kitchener-Waterloo Symphony greeted me with a massive umbrella. I was soaked and felt like a drowned rat. I arrived during intermission, with about five minutes to spare. Fortunately, Brian had arranged for a television in the hall, so the audience could see me in Ottawa. This turned out to be a good thing, because he had laryngitis and wasn't able to entertain with stories.

To great cheers, I sang in my gala gown, which was wet and still sewn on me. I explained this to the crowd, which made them laugh. The second night's show was not as dramatic. The reviews were exceptional, one headline reading, "Riki's royal date didn't keep her away." However, I wish I had been able to stay in Ottawa and enjoy the elegant supper that was served on the stage.

Later that summer of 1982, I learned how to play tennis. Asked to be on a CBC show called *Celebrity Tennis*, I told the producer that I had only used a racquet to drain spaghetti. He found this comical, but I said I was game to try anything new. I loved television and being on camera. The great part of this gig was that all the participants were guests of the Inn & Tennis Club at Manitou, which had a superb restaurant and picturesque accommodation on a lake in Parry Sound. We could bring along a guest, and all our meals as well as clothes and equipment would be gifted, as we didn't receive a fee.

There were hockey players, Olympic champions, mayor of Toronto Art Eggleton, other singers, and actors. It was a celebration. Robert came with me, and I became aware of his growing resentment of my success. He started to put me down in front of others, very subtly, but it had moved beyond the "your high note was sharp" type of comment. Nevertheless, he played tennis when we weren't shooting. The series continued for many years until someone at CBC realized that no one was watching the show, as it was pretty boring, and it was cancelled. I continued playing in Toronto, joined a club, and found the game a great release for tension, and later on for my anxiety and sorrow.

While we were away for our week on the courts, Carrie went to summer camp. She was booked to stay for a month but was sent home after two weeks when she was caught in a boy's cabin. Actually in his bunk. I hated losing the money for the camp fees for those two lost weeks. However, I wasn't terribly angry with her, because I had done something similar years before, but never was caught.

The incident turned out to be an opportunity to spend some summer time with my teenage daughter, and. I suggested a trip to France. I booked a rental apartment in the small town of Juan les Pins in the Riviera. The Canadian dollar was at an all-time high against the franc, so I reasoned that we would make money on the trip—my way of convincing Robert that we should go, just Carrie and me, that is.

We flew on Air France to Paris, then a cheap flight to Nice where our rental car awaited arrival. Our little Renault was manual, and I never could figure out how to get it into reverse. Everywhere we went was forward. The apartment I had reserved was in an ugly multi-unit complex. Fortunately, my handwriting on the contract was illegible, and our deposit did not go through. Change of plans. We were free to travel and stay where we liked. I am still a flexible traveller. What a grand time we had! We laughed at our good luck and giggled at the car always going forward.

Our first night in Nice, we stayed at a simple, no-frills hotel, ate dinner al fresco, and took pleasure in a warm evening walk on the quay. The following morning, we commenced the journey of discovery—of the Riviera and ourselves. The little car was bursting with our belongings. We both had two over-sized suitcases filled with outfits and shoes for every occasion. Our original plans had us in one place where we could unpack. We had everything with us, and I mean everything. I am a more efficient packer now.

We stayed at Le Mirabeau, a charming hotel between Monaco and Monte Carlo, chosen because it was on one side of a roundabout, which I kept circling until I could manoeuvre the Renault into the driveway. The valet was happy to take the car off our hands, even though I explained that the reverse gear didn't work—not easy in French. He grinned broadly.

We walked for hours some days and talked incessantly. We lay topless on the beach with all the other topless women, and it seemed natural to both of us. We dined in both casual and elegant restaurants. Carrie would always order beef tenderloin, with raspberries for dessert laid out flat in little rows. I would get a half bottle of gewürztraminer, and we would each have a glass. After dinner, she would politely ask if I minded if she smoked, and I would tell her to just go ahead but blow the smoke in the other direction. Everyone was smoking in those days, especially in France. I was just so elated to be with her, spending time together, I ignored her nasty habit. She could have been smoking cigars, and I wouldn't have complained.

Men flirted with both of us and, being French, they were very overt about their passes. One man asked if he could date my sister. As much as I was flattered, I turned him down. I was thirty-eight, and she was sixteen; I looked younger, and she looked older. One day, we separated just to see what it was like to be on our own. We both arrived back at the hotel early because we had missed each other.

The last two days, I splurged, and we stayed at the famous Negresco Hotel, where we were upgraded to a suite. It was unusual, then, to have fluffy terry robes in the room, but they were there, and we both wandered around in ours and sat on the balcony overlooking the Mediterranean. We felt like movie stars.

The final evening, we ate in the hotel's Michelin-starred restaurant, the Chantecler. I loved goat's milk cheese, still do, and picked a sample of every *chevre* on the *chariot*, the wheeled serving tray, filling my plate with about thirty different ones. A couple sitting at the next table remarked on my selection. It turned out they were from Toronto and lived only a few minutes from our house. I was to see them a great deal in the future.

In French restaurants in those days, rather than sitting two women at a corner table out of view as they did in Toronto, they sat us in the centre of the room. Both wearing black cocktail dresses, we must have made quite an impression—Carrie with her startling red hair and beautiful tawny face, and me with my long blond tresses. We were treated with great respect and admiration. It was a perfect conclusion to an extraordinary vacation. Best of all, Carrie and I now shared a much more intimate relationship.

Aria- song of a life

After our return, I planned a dinner party with a surprise guest Christopher Atkins, whom I had met in Hollywood in the spring. A fledgling movie star, he was appearing in *Blue Lagoon* with Brooke Shields. As substitute host of the *Summer Festival* series for CBC television, I was sent on a Hollywood junket to interview Shields and the rest of the cast. She had just turned fifteen, and Christopher was eighteen.

Aside from the interviews, my duties included attending a very smart dinner party at the home of the president of Columbia Pictures, Frank Price. I agonized over what to wear, with all the fashionable Hollywood people, and then decided on a sophisticated white satin suit with a short skirt and peplum jacket. As it turned out, I needn't have worried, because I was one of the best dressed. The only stars I recognized were Christopher Atkins, Brooke Shields, and the producer of the movie, Randal Kleiser.

Chasen's restaurant catered the food, which featured their famous chili. One of the waiters, most likely an aspiring actor, managed to spill a cup of it on my new suit. I rushed to the washroom to try to minimize the damage and bumped into Christopher. He was very sweet and tried to help me, then invited me back to his place for a nightcap. I turned him down, but we chatted playfully, and he mentioned that he would be visiting Toronto in the summer and would love to see me again.

I didn't really expect him to show up a dinner I was hosting. But he did, and made quite an entrance on our street in his stretch white limousine—not easy to drive down a short and narrow cul de sac. After we greeted each other with hugs, I noticed that Carrie was reduced to mush in his presence. I immediately realized how inappropriate it was for me to be flirting with him. I still have my *Blue Lagoon* beach towel and smile wistfully when I use it.

Around that time, I was sitting in a trendy Yorkville restaurant, Il Posto, beside someone who looked familiar. It was Sylvia Tyson, a well-known country singer/songwriter. We struck up a conversation, which ultimately led to collaboration with a third artist, Kathryn Moses, a jazz saxophonist, flute player, and singer. We developed the idea for a show featuring the three of us in concert, and sold the concept to Harbourfront Centre, an outdoor theatre that seated thousands. The concert highlighted each one of us alone, as well as the three of us combined. It seemed fitting to call it *Together*. We used Sylvia's band, and hired a few extra musicians who could play for me in the classical numbers.

I performed an opera sampler of excerpts of all the famous arias that featured a very high E-flat at the end, guaranteed to impress. Sylvia chose a selection of her well-known greatest hits, and Kathryn displayed her brilliance with jazz samplings on the sax and flute. We sang everything from the raunchy "Wild Women Don't Get No Blues" to "Three Little Maids from School" from *The Mikado*. We wrote one song that was accompanied by a rock beat, and we all played instruments and performed, "It Don't Mean a Thing if It Ain't Got That Swing." I borrowed a stand-up bass for that one—hadn't played since high school, but I practised, and it worked.

The designer Wayne Clarke lent us outfits, that were black and silver sequined. I had a skin-tight slinky long gown (which he insisted on giving to me, and it is still in my costume cupboard), and the other two wore figure-hugging pants with matching jackets, all different but coordinated. The newspapers contained articles about us cooking and modelling our clothes. We were a publicist's dream team, and we proved a smash.

The three of us spent a great deal of time together, and we melded. I had never had a supportive relationship with other women in the entertainment business who lived close by. I had many opera singer friends, but we were always at opposite ends of the country. I think Robert felt left out. He didn't have any male friends outside of work. I was his close companion. It was an adjustment for him when I arrived home at one o'clock in the morning, all giggly and talkative about my stimulating experiences with the girls, and I sensed he resented them.

One of the pop agents tried to woo me as a client, but his coke habit interfered. We could have done dozens of follow-up concerts, but Kathryn wanted to move to Los Angeles to try her luck there in the music market, so that was the end of that. The whole process was an eye-opener for me. It was such a different world from opera and symphony. The crossover aspect of the music was pleasurable and innovative but a trifle scary. I felt safer in my classical environment.

I had acquired a new appreciation of why women have girlfriends. I became more open to relationships with other women, rather than being competitive with them. I began spending more time with my sister and appreciating how lucky I was to have her in my life. She became my best friend.

Carrie seemed to have calmed down, though she was making noises about changing schools once again and going to a public high school.

I think it was the strict curriculum at TFS, and she was bored with being with rich kids all the time, or so she said. Her interest in fashion had grown, and she was starting to think about her future after she graduated. She was sketching clothes, putting together unusual outfits and spending time on Queen Street, visiting the retro clothing stores.

She loved her music, playing the electric bass, and occasionally singing in a band with Washington on keyboards and some other friends I don't remember. She biked all over downtown and was very independent. It was hard to keep up with her, but I certainly tried.

She was hired at CITY television to work on the new *MuchMusic* show, modelled after MTV, and a pretty happening place for a seventeen year old. Anne Howard, my new manager, who was becoming a good friend, along with her partner, Ellen Goldberg, was the producer. She promised to keep an eye on Carrie, whose record collection grew, and sounds of David Bowie, Stevie Wonder, and Prince mixed with Joan Sutherland, Beverly Sills, and Pavarotti.

I developed an interest in the music of Kurt Weill that went beyond "Mack the Knife" and *The Three Penny Opera*. I studied his life and his chameleon-like composing in different styles, as he moved from Germany to France and finally to America. Lewis Brown, who had designed the costumes for Curley's Wife in Amsterdam, sent me old tapes of Weill's music, songs I had never heard before. I visited the library at the Faculty of Music and went digging. I found some unusual repertoire from all Weill's periods and decided to put together a concert of this material.

I came upon a unique work—*The Seven Deadly Sins*, which Weill had written for soprano, orchestra, and a dancer. Boris Brott programmed this, and we performed it in a few concerts, one of which was recorded by CBC radio in Winnipeg. I felt drawn to this work with its dark disturbing music. When we first did the piece, it was only with orchestra, but we were invited to perform it at the Stratford Festival.

A dancer/choreographer was hired, as well as a director. It was one of the weirdest experiences of my performing career. The dancer, Anne Ditchburn, was a mesmerizing creature, who had been in a few arty films. She floated around, and was quite entrancing, and beautiful in an ephemeral way, but there was an unsavoury side to her. She was always very nice to me, but she was wretched to work with. She never completed the choreography and drove our director, Richard Ouzounian, crazy. She was involved intimately with the designer and, although I was not privy to the details, I sensed it was a destructive relationship.

The work went well musically, but the rehearsals were filled with tension and frustration. The performance took place with a great deal of improvisation, which wasn't the intention, because Anne was not fully prepared. On the positive side, I became close with Richard, a friendship that has endured for many years.

Weill's music haunted me, and I began to think about doing a recording of his work, reflecting all his musical styles. In Germany, there was his connection with Brecht and *The Three Penny Opera*, among many other works. He was Jewish, and in the 1930s left Germany and relocated to France, where he wrote in the French idiom. Since anti-Semitism lurked there as well—an understatement at best, he headed to New York. There, he wrote in the American idiom. "September Song" was one of the most popular of this genre.

Lotte Lenya, Weill's widow, had passed away a few years earlier, but the Kurt Weill Foundation, which she established in New York in 1962, was receptive to my idea of a recording of Weill's music, and I needed their permission. Fortunately, I had already established a good reputation in the business, so they gave me not only their authorization but also their blessing. I spent a few months exploring and choosing the repertoire, and gathered together a small chamber ensemble to accompany me, led by jazz pianist Doug Riley. I signed a contract with a small record label Fanfare, and we set a date for early May in 1985.

Meanwhile, Carrie switched schools for her final year to Leaside High School, and was determined to apply to either the Fashion Institute of Technology or Parsons School of Design in New York. I thought it would be wise to visit the schools. Washington had broken up with Carrie, and she was quite miserable, so the New York trip would work on many levels. Although she didn't get over him, she was distracted, and we managed to have a really good time.

Parsons School appealed most because the marketing side of fashion interested her. We also felt that she had a better chance of getting accepted there. She was good at drawing, but she was brilliant about trends and style in fashion.

We stayed near Central Park, and went everywhere. Soho held an attraction for her, and we bought some funky clothes in artsy boutiques. Little red flatties/ballerina slippers, appealed. So did a T-shirt by a company called Parachute with a picture of Grace Jones and one by Fiorucci with a girl floating in the air, both of which I still have.

I booked tickets to a revival of *West Side Story*. When I was crying, I peeked over at her and noticed tears trickling down her face. We went to *Cats*, which Carrie loved. I did a bit of snoozing during the performance until one of the actors arrived on the balcony near us and startled me awake. We ate in diners, talked and planned. Carrie's future was starting to look very promising.

Things were not so pleasant in my marriage. Everything on the surface seemed fine, but it wasn't, and I was about to turn forty. That was a very daunting prospect for me, and I was taking stock of my life. Robert was still critical about everything in music. Nothing ever measured up, and it wasn't just my performances with which he found fault. The critic was just a part of who he was. If he didn't like an opera, we would get up and leave, and everyone would notice because we had seats in full view and were well known. A public statement was made by our actions, and it was not a nice one. He continued putting me down in front of dinner guests. I had developed into a self-reliant and confident woman. I looked in the mirror one day and said to my image, "You are still marketable, and this is not working. Do something."

In July of that year,1983, Princess Diana and Prince Charles were coming to Canada, and there was a summer barbecue arranged near Ottawa. I was thrilled to be attending with many other artists, performers, and Canadian celebrities. The event took place on the glorious lawns of Governor General Edward Shreyer's summer residence. It was a balmy evening, and I wore a summery off-the-shoulder, mid-calf, white eyelet cotton dress, with a polka-dot red and white sash. Diana wore a blue frock and low-heeled shoes and no stockings—possibly the first time that a Royal was dressed so casually, with bare tanned legs displayed for all to see.

We were seated at round tables under a tent, with some of us fortunate to be in a separate area with Diana and Charles. In fact, she was seated close to me at the next table, with Pierre Trudeau. Prince Charles was at a different table, but close to hers and mine. I was next to Conrad Black, the newspaper magnate, who was a mesmerizing dinner companion and who seemed to know all about me, very smooth and unsettling. We talked about my latest project, Kurt Weill's music, and he knew all about Weill, particularly the prewar period in Germany, and conversed in great detail. Little did I know then I would be a future investor in his Hollinger companies, lose money, and end up living in Florida, not terribly far from Coleman Prison, where he spent some time. Life's little coincidences.

Diana and I chatted briefly about opera and ballet, and she was well informed. She asked which roles I had sung. I mentioned my favourite, Musetta, in *La Boheme,* and she remarked that visually I suited the character. She found the opera touching and sad. But she said that she had more of an affinity for ballet.

She and Prince Charles seemed full of love and smiled secretively at one another throughout the meal. It is hard to believe she was only twenty-one; she celebrated her twenty-second birthday on the tour during Klondike Days in Edmonton. The food was typical summer barbecue buffet. We lined up for steak or salmon, corn on the cob, and baked potatoes. Afterward, many of us went to the Chateau Laurier Hotel bar and hung out chatting and drinking until very late. A glossy coffee table book was published of the Royal Tour. I can been seen with a big smile on my face, at the barbecue, a nice memento.

Beyond being the title of the famous book, 1984 was the year Trudeau resigned from politics, the Apple computer and mini-vans were born, and my fortieth birthday arrived. My sister threw a fabulous party for me at the Royal Ontario Museum. With her usual innovative flare, she had it catered with food that had never before been eaten in Toronto, like tricoloured pasta. The invitations were imaginative, on one side were the names of all the movie stars—including Farrah Fawcett, Raquel Welch, Jacqueline Bisset, and Candice Bergen—who were my age, and on the other, the words "Riki's joining the club". The party was overflowing with my friends and associates, as well as many of my sister's.

That was the beginning of marking birthdays with a big celebration. Carol and I decided that we should embrace the years as milestones, a tradition that has continued to this day. The after-party pictures show me sitting with Carrie at home, opening presents, with Robert off to the side. I do not look particularly happy, and he looks sulky. That was February.

In April, I went to Vancouver, sang Mendelssohn's *Elijah,* and visited with Juliette, who had become a close friend and confidante. We talked about Robert and our marriage. Juliette told me, "You will find a third man who will be the great love of your life. Don't be afraid to leave Robert. It will be better for him, too. You will see."

That conversation kick-started my decision. And as usual for me, it didn't take long to move on a plan; however, I wanted to talk to Carrie about it first. I told her straight out that I wanted to leave Robert, and that it wouldn't affect her relationship with him. I said that, as she knew, he was considerably older than I and that my energy level was higher. I wanted to do more, and our relationship had run its course. I still cared for him and would always have love for him. She said, "I totally understand, Mom. You want to boogie out, and Robert is happy watching TV and going to concerts."

She warned me that if I found another man, to be sure that he was reliable and didn't keep me waiting and stand me up when something better came along. She was referring to Gary, a very likable and caring friend of mine who always kept me and everyone else waiting in restaurants. He would phone from his car and apologize, but he was always frustratingly late.

When I returned to Toronto, Robert and I went out to dinner at Statländer's very new restaurant. I was nervous, but it didn't stop me from enjoying an inventive meal, with fresh ingredients from local farms, unusual in Toronto at that time. We talked about my trip out West, the food, and then our relationship. I broached the idea of splitting. This wasn't the first time, but whenever I brought up the subject he dismissed it with, "You don't have the nerve."

I told him that I thought our marriage was stagnating; that we were at different places in our lives since I had just turned forty; that I was at a personal juncture in my development, and that I wanted to move on. I didn't say that we never laughed anymore, or that he put me down in front of friends, or that we both had affairs, and I wasn't happy. I did say that we both took each other for granted, and that I thought he would be happier without me. I don't think he really believed I would go through with it. He responded, "You'll never be able to support yourself and Carrie." I told him that I didn't want anything from him, except to keep the house, but he could take anything he wanted from the house, and I would help him find a place to live. He could have the car with my licence plates that said RIKI T.

I continued that Carrie loved him very much—he had to know this—and would spend as much time with him as the two of them wanted. Tigger, along with the frozen crunchy smelts, a light-hearted touch, would stay with us. I felt sorrowful telling Robert all this, despite my little joke. We made it through dinner, ignoring the looks from the diners right beside us. I didn't want to cry in the restaurant and knew we would try to be civil to one another. And we were. It wasn't long before we reached a legal agreement.

I was booked to do a show in musical theatre, performing every night, and I knew I could buy a small car with my earnings. I purchased a Renault Sport with a semi-soft top that pushed back, almost like a convertible. It was shiny black, very attractive, and cost $5,000 cash brand new.

My brother-in-law, Bernie, offered to hire Carrie on weekends to do some office work, and said he would pay her a small salary that would cover her expenses. On her eighteenth birthday, she lost her support from Mort. I was confident that the work would continue to come in, as it had done for the past fourteen years, and we would be just fine financially. I had the English painting that my parents bought years ago because the model looked like my sister, *Gossips by the Roadside*. Carol didn't want it, and I could sell it if I needed an infusion of cash at any time.

Robert stayed at the house while I looked for a place for him to live. Once I found something suitable, I took him there. It was a charming townhouse in a developing area downtown, just west of Bathurst Street off King. The model was in his colours, red and black, and that clinched it. It was fully furnished and snazzy. I convinced the owner of the development to sell Robert that particular unit.

He couldn't move for a few months until the other townhouses were purchased, as they used his as a showcase. We lived together, knowing we would be splitting. We ate together as usual, and slept together as well, as there were only the two beds in the house, and Carrie was in the other. Civility was the order of the day, and being British, Robert seemed content with this modus operandi. Perhaps he thought I might change my mind, but I knew I wouldn't. The cause for our divorce was stated as marriage breakdown. The agreement was simple and straightforward. Of course, these things are never totally pleasant, but I felt released and renewed.

Robert started dating all sorts of women, including a workout guru on CITY television, who was renowned for saying, "You can do it, just one more time..." as she bounced around with her neat little body. He dated a black pianist whom I knew and liked—ironic as he had made a fuss about Washington being black. I was relieved he was dating. I didn't feel as guilty about the divorce. While he was still at the house—this lasted for two months, I went out with other women, an older platonic male friend, and my gay friends.

I wasn't interested in anything except earning money. I went to the banker to get the mortgage reworked, and it turned out he was an ardent fan. In those days, the banking profession did not treat women very well, especially if they didn't have a nine-to-five job. So I was fortunate. Carrie spent time with Robert. They went out to dinner and to a ballet. They managed brilliantly. I never asked her what they discussed, just trusted that she was mature enough at eighteen to handle the new situation. My job calendar filled up, and we were set.

The musical I was hired to do was actually at a cabaret theatre The Teller's Cage. I would be singing every evening—a departure for an opera singer, as we normally performed only every few nights. The piece was a Rodgers and Hammerstein musical for four singers, called *Some Enchanted Evening*. It included some dialogue joining musical numbers and minimal dancing. One singer was Christopher Holder, a hunky guy from *The Young and The Restless* television soap opera, charming and very professional. And we didn't date.

Every day, I would have a ten-minute nap just before six o'clock, eat one hundred grams of pasta, and drive downtown to the show, singing along to Lionel Richie tapes, in my new little car, René, a French name for a French car. The performances were well attended and enjoyable. I would head home after eleven.

Robert finally moved to his new place, and I started to date some men from my tennis club and some who'd heard from my sister that I was on the market. But mostly, I enjoyed my new freedom. I didn't have to worry about pleasing Robert and living up to his expectations. I didn't have to hear his criticisms of other artists. Everything was just so positive during the day. I could do what I wanted to do, when I wanted to do it. Carrie was grown up, and we lived together harmoniously. A weight had been lifted from my shoulders.

Robert took almost nothing from the house, as his new place was completely furnished. He had no room for his enormous record collection of at least a thousand LPs, but I told him he could have them whenever he moved somewhere larger or whenever he wanted them. They are still with me. We were divorced in 1984, and he eventually moved to

Vancouver, after the tragedy. It was strange seeing him leave the house with the car and my name on the plate.

I never felt I made a mistake. I hoped Robert would find future happiness with someone else, and he did in time marry a beautiful Asian woman half his age. She had two sons by a previous marriage, and Robert took them on happily. From time to time, we have lunch when I am in Vancouver and talk mostly about music. None of our friends seemed to take sides. I tried hard to mend some relationships at the Canadian Opera Company after we had walked out so many times during performances that it became a statement. I am a now good friend with the management and a strong supporter of the company, but it took work.

Riki greeting Queen Elizabeth backstage at National arts Centre, Ottawa, Photo credit, official publicity still, Canadian Press 1982

Aria- song of a life

Titania, Midsummer Night's Dream, Ottawa with Countertenor John York-Skinner, photo credit:official publicity still National Arts Centre 1978

Violetta, Canadian Opera Company, tenor Paul Frey, photo credit: official publicity still Canadian Opera Company 1978

Riki Turofsky

Before interview with a very young Brooke Shields
(candid snapshot by collegue)

Lamento—Sorrowful Time 1985

Carrie was in her last year of high school. Her application for Parsons was in the mail, but she wouldn't hear until the early spring. She spent time with her friends and with me. We enjoyed a quiet Christmas at Anne Howard and Ellen Goldberg's home in Rosedale, practically around the corner. Anne was no longer my business manager, but we remained close, and Ellen was her soulmate and partner. Carrie and I adored them.

New Year's Eve 1985 arrived without much fanfare. I don't even remember what I did or whom I was with. Carrie went out with her gang. She and I had made a deal that she wouldn't date anyone over thirty, and I wouldn't date anyone under thirty. I think we both broke it and laughed at our silliness. Carrie was fast developing into a very beautiful young woman, both inside and out. She adopted stray friends, whom I would find sleeping on the living-room couch or in the den. She had many pals, was a good listener, and still was attached to her music, often dressing up to go to *The Rocky Horror Picture Show* that always seemed to be in revival. She was in high spirits.

I started dating different types of men—lawyers, accountants, businessmen, developers, even a photographer. One evening, I went out with an earnest and brilliant young man named Ned, who was working on his PhD and definitely under thirty. We went to a movie. While he went to the washroom, I went to buy the popcorn. I loved popcorn smothered in butter, but when I arrived at the counter, I was told that they had started using a new product called Golden Topping. There was a man beside me in line, and the two of us started talking about this appalling turn of events. He loved butter, too. Ned returned, and we went into the theater.

That was in February. In March, Carrie wasn't feeling well, and I took her to the doctor. I met my sister for lunch at a new restaurant called the Westside Grill, and we were seated beside two men, one who looked vaguely familiar. He said that we had met at a movie theatre over popcorn butter. I remembered the conversation but not him. He was not my type particularly, quite fair and preppy looking, and seemed like a yuppie. His friend, Rod, was very smooth and, before long he had my phone number, using some excuse about knowing a mutual friend. I was very distracted and anxious to pick Carrie up from school. She had wanted to return after missing the morning at the doctor's. She seemed better when I saw her later.

It was an unusually warm spring. My sister invited us for traditional Passover dinner, the second night, which that year fell on Carrie's nineteenth birthday, April 6. It was a Saturday, and after the *Seder*, Carrie left to celebrate with friends. She came home late, but had called as usual to let me know it would be after midnight.

On Sunday, she complained that she wasn't feeling well once again. By Monday, she was sick with diarrhea and vomiting. When I called her doctor, I was told it was most likely the flu, and the symptoms would pass. They didn't. She became sicker. I took her to Mount Sinai Hospital Monday afternoon, where she was put on intravenous, although they had trouble with her veins and had to reinsert the needle numerous times. Carrie stayed in emergency until Friday. She was given some very strong medicine, and was feeling much better and begged to be released. They were not certain which virus had caused the trouble, but she had responded quite well to the antibiotics, although not completely. She couldn't wait to get home and wash her hair.

I had a first date booked for that Saturday, April 13, with a man I had recently met. He was president of a major advertising agency and quite sophisticated. I was looking forward to the evening. Carrie seemed to have made a good recovery, but was still weak and had lost weight; she was slim to begin with. She asked if she could borrow my cute little Renault for the evening to visit one of her friends in the east end for a sleepover.

After she left, I found a dozen pink roses with a note from her that simply said, "I love you. See you tomorrow." She often did thoughtful things, but this was special. I think it stemmed from the fact that I lent her the car and trusted her to keep it overnight. I still have the card. The weather was balmy, and I knew she would open the soft top of the car to enjoy the sunlight. She looked good in that little black automobile. Somewhere I have a picture of her in it, with a big smile on her face.

My date, Ev Elting, arrived, and we went to a local restaurant on Avenue Road, not far from my place. Dinner was excellent, and our conversation ranged widely. He was urbane and erudite, had a dry wit, and knew his food and wine. He was attractive, not tall, but he drove a sexy Jaguar. I was having a fine time and thought that this was a relationship worth pursuing. We weren't out late, and planned to meet again. I went to bed looking forward to hearing from him. I fell fast asleep around midnight.

At first I slept well, but woke suddenly and found myself breathless. I saw that it was three-thirty in the morning on my clock radio. I smiled when I remembered what a good evening I had spent. There was some light outside in the mess of tangled trees that I could see from my window, but that wasn't what woke me. I was upset by something. I knew that Carrie was at her girlfriend's overnight, but I couldn't stop thinking about her. I took some deep breaths, and managed to get back to sleep until I felt Tigger's rough tongue on my cheek and knew that it was time to get up.

It was a beautiful Sunday morning and, opening the sliding glass doors to my small balcony, I noticed how really warm it was, like a summer's morn. I freshened up, put on a robe, and went downstairs to deal with the cat's breakfast and retrieve the *Globe and Mail* from the front step. I made a cup of decaf, still thinking about my Saturday evening. I was just getting comfortable when the doorbell rang. My heart skipped a few beats, as I wasn't expecting anyone so early on a Sunday. I went to open it.

Two very tall policemen were standing in front of me. I felt sick to my stomach. I knew what they were going to say before they said it. I couldn't hear their words. Horrible words. The most horrific words any parent could ever hear. The words we all fear from the moment of birth. I missed the part when they asked me if I was Carrie's mother, but I heard the part when they said, "We are sorry to have to tell you that your daughter died at 3:30 this morning."

They started to relate the details, but I couldn't understand what they were saying, except that I should phone someone close to me, and get them to come over. I will stop writing for a few minutes; I can't see through the tears as I summon the memories.

We went into my bright happy yellow kitchen that should have been sombre and dark. I found the phone, or maybe they found it, and I called my sister. Somehow I remembered that she was at her farm in Caledon for the weekend. When I heard her voice, the words fell out of my mouth. "Carrie's dead!"

Carol said something like, "I can't get there for an hour. I will call someone to be with you immediately." Within minutes my sister's nephew, Norman, who was also our doctor, arrived and wrapped me in his arms. I can't remember when the screaming started, maybe after the police left. I was told later on that I could be heard everywhere on the street. My opera singer lungs were in full force and, combined with my anguish, it must have been a cacophony. The screams became sobs, and the house filled with people.

The Whites arrived, and Sally and Neil, my sister and Bernie. Tigger, who was a pristine cat, made a mess on the floor in Carrie's room. I can't remember much after that. Somehow we found out what had happened to Carrie, and were to ascertain more as the week went on when the autopsy report came in. Did it matter? Carrie was dead and I wanted to be.

The funeral had to be arranged, along with the cemetery and all the gruesome details. My sister was in a state of focus and calm, as she had been after our mother had died, although I am sure she was distraught inside like the rest of us. In the Jewish tradition, the burial must take place as quickly as possible, but I thought we should wait until Mort arrived in Toronto from out West. It was hard to find him for some reason, but he could get to Toronto by Tuesday. Always late.

The *shiva* would be at my house. My sister called Carol Lang in Vancouver, Carrie's old babysitter and my longtime friend, and asked her to come and stay with me. My sister would pay the airfare. Bernie told me that he would identify Carrie's body, saying, "Remember her alive and laughing, not frozen in time." That was good advice. Bernie asked if we would donate Carrie's eyes. As an ophthalmologist, he was aware of the great need. I agreed. Carrie had signed a donor card on her driver's licence, so that was her wish. All these details kept me from thinking.

My car had to be retrieved from the house of Carrie's friend Samantha, and that was dealt with by somebody. My sister called Benjamin's Park Memorial funeral home. Michael was the boss now, my old pal from West Prep, and we went to see him. He was soothing. There were so many things going on in a short time. I will describe them, but they are most likely out of sequence.

My sister, Carol, stayed with me that first night (there are so many Carols in my life), and we both liked to sleep on the right side of the bed. I won out on that one. The Vancouver Carol arrived and started to help with her zany sense of humour. She was legally blind and, watching her load the dishwasher was quite a sight. The cemetery was to be a new one in Maple, Ontario, where wild deer roamed, called Pardes Shalom, or Park of Peace. It appealed.

I was not a religious Jew, but the rituals meant a lot to me at that time, something to hold onto in my grief, which was terrifying. A cardinal flew into the yard, and I was sure it was Carrie in some new guise. My sister and I both interpreted this as a sign from her, with her red hair. Cardinals were to play an important part in soothing me in my grief, then and now. The pink roses she had given me were still alive; but she wasn't. The pink roses, too, would play a supportive role in the future. Any symbol of her became meaningful.

Men called *shomers* would sit with her body from the time of death until the funeral, reciting psalms to protect her spirit. I chose an unadorned casket without nails, and she was washed in a *mikvah* or purifying bath, then wrapped in a shroud. I decided that my nephew, Jordan, who adored Carrie, would be the speaker at the service. It was still very hot. Carrie would have loved the weather. I spoke to Ev, who had daughters, and even though I hardly knew him, he was an ear and a comfort to me.

Mort arrived with earrings he had bought for Carrie for her birthday; as always too late. His first birthday gift for her arrived after her death. Robert was distraught and needed companionship.

The funeral was tragic. The sun was shining on all of us in our black suits. It was still very hot on April 14. The coffin was covered in pink roses, sent by my sister's best friend. The chapel was filled with young and old, and Jordy acquitted himself well. I can't remember a word. I just cried through it all, but he wrote beautifully then and still does today. The music, which always heightens emotions, made us cry even more. I chose music that Carrie liked—Prince and a Jewish lullaby I had sung, and other pieces that Anne and Ellen had gathered, and put together on a tape.

The cemetery was in the country and somehow serene. I spotted Ev off to the side and many of my dear friends. Afterwards, my little house on Bishop Street was bursting with people, eating and drinking, and crying and laughing.

When Carrie died, I was told she had a drug overdose, aspirated her vomit, stopped breathing, and been rushed to East General Hospital. I assumed she and her friends were smoking pot and perhaps experimented with some other drugs; as she had just left the hospital and was on heavy drugs from there, everything would have been magnified. I did not know the details, nor was I told them by her friends. I do have a vague recollection of them telling me something, but the trauma of it all made it difficult to comprehend what was going on.

It has been years since I could recall any salient details from that time—almost twenty-five, when I allowed myself to try to remember anything, and to start writing this book. Carrie had needle marks in her arm, and this is what the paramedics misinterpreted. These marks were the result of the intravenous needles she had been given at Mount Sinai during her hospitalization the previous week, when they had trouble finding a vein.

When I was sitting *shiva* at my house after the funeral, I received a call from the coroner. I had requested an autopsy. I remember taking the phone in the kitchen and shushing everyone so I could hear what he had to say. The underlying cause of death was not drug related. They had found evidence of *E. coli* bacteria in her stomach. She had left the hospital too soon when they were trying to find out what was causing her illness, and she had been on intravenous a week previously. *E. coli* had not been diagnosed at that time. For some reason in 1985, even after she had been to Mexico during the summer, they did not check for this horrendous bug.

She had choked on her own vomit, aspirated, and died of a pulmonary edema, her lungs filled with fluid, and she couldn't breathe and was rushed to the hospital. I do not know when her friends called for an ambulance; I do not know the particulars except that she was pronounced dead at 3:30 am, the time I awoke suddenly. I didn't want to know the particulars, which might seem peculiar. I didn't spend time thinking that if she had been home could I have saved her? What good would that do?

Some parents go to great lengths to know everything. For me, it was sufficient to know what I learned from the coroner. No blame to anyone. She was dead, and couldn't be brought back no matter what I did or knew. I was now a member of the worst club, parents who lost a child. To this day, when I meet someone who has been through this unnatural event, we understand each other instantly; we understand the horror.

A despicable little man called Jocko Thomas, a *Toronto Star* reporter who hung out at the city morgue, spread the rumour of a drug death, and some papers carried the story, as I was a celebrity. After they were alerted of the mistake and printed an apology, that little bit of news died. I found the home phone number of Mr. Thomas, whom I referred to as a bottom feeder, and called him in the middle of the night to tell him what I thought of him. My father must have known him, and I threw that in for good measure. It gave me some consolation. I was angry at the world and God and at that despicable little man, who died in 2010 at 96.

The good thing about the Jewish religion, which I was suddenly fervently adopting, was the tradition of *shiva*. It had a rhythm. Every day, Carol Lang and I would get up and clean the front room for the onslaught of visitors. Carrie had made two huge photo albums, which sat on the coffee table, giving us a focus for talking about her accomplishments, along with photos, documenting her life.

Prayers were said only in the evening. There was food, continuously delivered from friends, and friends of friends. Flowers were everywhere, and there were many donations to charities. Robert came, stayed, and ate, and I think he was hoping he could come back permanently. Mort stayed for the funeral. He was self-contained. I could hardly look at him. I knew he was devastated, especially because he had tried to reach out to her with a gift for the first time, for her birthday, which was one week before.

I was in a daze. I decided that when *shiva* week was finished, I would go to synagogue to learn Hebrew and become a devout Jew. Carrie's friends were everywhere, mostly hanging out in her room. One of Carrie's best buddies, Karl, wanted to stay over and sleep on the sofa. He was so lost, I couldn't say no; but after a week, I had to ask him to leave. I can't remember specifically who else was there every day. I am sure one was Shelley Boylen, Carrie's best friend. My sister and Bernie, Sari and Jordy, the Whites, Sally and Neil, and all my sister's family and parades of people came each day as well. Anne and Ellen put me to bed every night.

Long desperate hugs were the order of the day, and masses of food that I liked. Our doctor asked what he could send, and I requested Chinese food. Corned beef and other deli products filled my fridge—comfort foods all.

Carol Lang stayed through it all. My other Carol friend, Carol Kirsh, was there. My neighbour and friend Catherine Williams, who held the fort and watched my house during the funeral, continued to be sensitively supportive. Maureen Forrester, a dear colleague who lived around the corner on Hazleton Avenue, arrived with apple cake she had just baked. And so on....

My buddy Gary Walker suggested that I go on a sailing trip with him and an assortment of his ex-girlfriends for Race Week in Antigua at the end of April, with Gary looking after all my costs. He convinced me that it would be good to get away, especially out on the water. I had just started my classes at the synagogue, but made the not-so-difficult choice to go on the trip. That was the end of my Jewish rehabilitation.

The day after *shiva* ended, a letter came in the mail from Parsons School in New York. They were pleased to offer Carrie a space in their program.

Carrie Turofsky Doran died April 14, 1985

Continuo—Life Goes On 1985–1987

Shiva was over, Carol Lang was heading back to Vancouver, people had cleared out of my house, and I was getting ready for a sailing trip to Antigua. Shelley came over, and we attacked the thank-you notes for all the flowers, donations, and dinners that people had sent. We sat in the garden and wept.

Carrie was gone. The house was empty.

Gary dropped by to give me a very small soft carry-on bag bearing the logo of his sailboat. He said that absolutely everything I was planning to take on the sailing trip had to fit into it. He mentioned that some guy would call to arrange a pick up for me on the morning of the departure. This person was the chef on board. As it was a forty-eight-foot sailboat, Gary said only some of us would sleep on board, while others would be in an adjacent motel. Apparently, there would be fifteen of us, nine of whom were his ex-girlfriends.

I was in a bewildered state as I shopped for some white resort clothing—shorts, pants, T-shirts, and sandals. Nothing special, except a jeweled T-shirt that I really liked. All would fit in the little waterproof bag. The next day, I had a call from this strange guy, who I thought was the chef on board. "Perhaps we can go out for a dinner or something," he said. "It was nice that you waved at me on the Gardiner Expressway yesterday. When I saw your licence plate with your name on it, I realized it was you, so I got your number from my friend, Rod."

I didn't have a clue what he was talking about. I told him, "My daughter just died, and I have been in my house sitting *shiva* for the last week. I don't drive on the Gardiner, and my name is not on my plate. I thought you were calling with the details about the sailing trip. What are you calling about, and who are you?"

"I met you in the Westside Grill about a month ago at lunch. You were with your sister, and you left to take your daughter to the doctor. Rod, my friend who sat beside you, got your number when you talked about a mutual friend. I met you previously in the movie theatre, where we discussed butter on popcorn. When I saw someone on the Gardiner in a white Transam with RIKKI on the plate and that person waved, I was sure it was you. Obviously, I was wrong. I am very sorry to hear about your daughter." He paused. "Would you consider going out for a drink?"

I started to get impatient. "Some friends are taking me to Race Week in Antigua for ten days. If you like, you can call when I return." I put the receiver down. I had only a vague recollection of the incidents, but none at all about him. He said his name was Chuck, a name I really detested.

I was in a zombie state for the trip. I didn't feel alone, since one of the others on board had lost his wife and job because of his drinking, and was seriously trying to give up alcohol. He had been on the boat for awhile and was doing well. What a place to try not to drink! It was a party all the time. Paul took me under his wing, becoming a friend in need. He protected me like an older brother.

The other women were fine. Everyone was pleasant. Gary was wooing a new girlfriend, who was extremely attractive, but it didn't seem to be going well. The actual races were exhilarating. I wasn't much of a sailor, but I took my Gravol anti-sea-sickness pills regularly and didn't have to contend with that misery.

There were many men on the other boats, so we fraternized quite a bit. Certainly, if women were looking to find men, a sailboat race was a good place to start, with a ratio of about twenty-to-one. I was charmed by an elegant man from Bermuda, a diversion until he divulged that he was married. When I split with Robert, my one rule was no married men.

Then, I met a Sam Shepard type of guy from a rich family in upper New York State. He was sexy and mysterious, and seemed to understand how sad and lost I was. He introduced me to a wise native woman, who told me, "Your daughter is in a better place. We all get on the bus, and then get off at different stops." For some reason, those words helped. He took me to a friend's house on the island for dinner one night, and I wore my sparkly T-shirt. He looked at me and said, "You are beautiful. You don't need to wear flashy clothes, just simple ones. Allow yourself to be the focus." I never wore it again, and I still wear simple clothes with good lines.

Aria- song of a life

I had an abundance of sun, sea air, and relaxation, and then the ten days were over. I returned to an empty house, except for Tigger, who had been looked after by a neighbour. I climbed into bed, pulled the covers over my head, and let my sadness engulf me. I lay there for about an hour, and then the damn phone rang. It was that ridiculous Chuck asking me out. He wanted to take me to hear a Vancouver singer, who was appearing in town and who happened to be the woman that Robert had been with when I had my car accident.

"No, I am not free and not interested." I hung up the phone. After a few minutes, I called him back to apologize for my rudeness and to ask for a rain check. We set a date for dinner later that week. I wandered listlessly around the house, called my sister and a few other friends, and tried to figure out my future without my daughter. There was a ton of mail, more condolence cards and so much to deal with, but I was frozen in my grief.

Religious feelings had definitely passed, but one flyer advertising grief counselling appealed to me. So I signed up with Bereaved Families of Ontario, a nonprofit organization that provides support to parents who have lost a child, and put that on my calendar.

Then there was the problem of going into Carrie's room. I called Anne and Ellen, and they offered to come over every night, bring a nice bottle of white wine, and tuck me in. The wine turned out to be Meursault, which did a very good job of putting me to sleep and spoiling me. They suggested that one of them should be with me when I sorted through Carrie's closet and that I should ask Shelley to be there, too, as Carrie's oldest friend. We set a date.

I did not want to sing ever again. I was in the middle of making the Kurt Weill recording and struggled to imagine finishing it. I knew it wouldn't be easy, but I had already committed most of it to memory, so I decided to complete the project. Doug Riley, the pianist-arranger and a fine jazz musician, had handpicked the chamber orchestra. It had to be a group that could move easily from the German and French periods of Weill's music to his Broadway show tunes like "September Song".

We recorded in the Flora McCrea Auditorium at Timothy Eaton Memorial Church, where the acoustics, although very live, were clean. The one song that would be performed only with piano, we decided to leave to another day for just Doug and me. I was well rehearsed and pleased with the results when we listened to the playbacks. My voice was fresh and, because there was no audience, I was able to concentrate on singing, despite the way I felt; the hollowness, despair, anguish, and loneliness that penetrated my soul. It was the beginning of June, almost two months since Carrie's death. Focusing on the job at hand helped me to keep going.

Doug and I set about to record the one piece with solo piano—"Lost in the Stars" from the musical of the same name, based on the book *Cry the Beloved Country*. It is a sombre and melancholy song, very simple and hauntingly beautiful. It took on a new meaning for me after Carrie's death, because some stranger had sent me a note that said I should think of Carrie as a gentle star that looked down upon the things of earth. The song talks about little stars like grains of sand in the palm of God's hands and one little star fell alone. I kept thinking about Carrie when I sang this line. Later on there is a line "Sometimes it seems maybe God's gone away, forgetting his promise..."

At this point, I really wondered if I could make it through. When I was younger, I used to think that God was finished with me. He took my father, then my mother. I thought to myself, *Okay, I'm safe now, no more bad things are going to happen.* But I was wrong. That doesn't seem to be the way life works itself out. So, there we were, just Doug and me, and I had to start. I looked at him and said, "This is going to be hard. Forgive me, if I break down."

He looked up from the music and said, "I understand. I lost a child as well." Then we did the piece without a blemish. You can hear our sorrow in the performance. "Lost in the Stars" became the final selection on the album.

The day for my date with the strange guy called Chuck arrived. I couldn't remember what he looked like and imagined he was probably balding and fair, not particularly good-looking. He arrived at my door, all perky, and talkative and smelling of some awful aftershave. He wasn't bald. In fact, he looked like a Kennedy, with his thick reddish brown hair and square face. I blurted out that I hated perfume on men. Good start. Shrugging that off, he led me to his yuppie blue BMW sedan.

We went to Marcel's, a rather nice French restaurant on King Street, where he chatted on and on about himself and his kids—three young boys of three, five, and seven, named Corby, Niels, and James, and how he was very separated from his wife. Niels was a Danish family name, as was his last name, Petersen. His children were everything to him. He was enthusiastic about life, and he listened to my stories. I didn't go on much about Carrie, except that I was going to go through her room and closet with my friends the following week and wasn't looking forward to it. I told him she had given me pink roses on the day of her death.

Chuck was not an opera fan. In fact, he had never been to one. He liked symphonic music and plays. He seemed cultured enough for one evening, at any rate. He enjoyed good wines. He was a sailor and a member of the Royal Canadian Yacht Club, but he was tired of competing. He was an avid cyclist and about to embark on a bike trip to France with a girlfriend. *What on earth is this fellow doing taking me out, if he is involved enough with someone, to take her to France on a trip?* Nevertheless, he booked to see me when he returned. I was less than enthusiastic.

I was hoping that my relationship with Ev would work out. He had been such a dear friend and support throughout the early tragic days. When I saw him that weekend after my Chuck date, he told me how much he liked me, but that he was in love with a woman he had met just before me. We had a few dates, but the excitement was definitely gone.

I went to New York to visit a man with whom I had played tennis in Toronto. He was quite boring, but I thought a New York trip might be good. I bought some angel-hair pasta that couldn't be found in Toronto in those days and some other goodies.

I was passing time. The meeting with the Bereaved Group wasn't the right thing for me. It was too sad hearing about everyone else's losses, when I was interested only in my own. I was restless, wondering about my future, when the phone rang. I was offered a position with CBC-TV in Vancouver. The head of regional television there, Ron Devion, had been highly supportive of my on-air television career. He had been transferred, heard about Carrie, and wondered if I wanted to relocate to host a few arts shows. Gratified, I said yes.

The day arrived to deal with Carrie's room. I had seen movies and television shows about parents who had lost a child and left their room exactly as they were when the child died. I could understand the fervent hope that it was all a mistake and the child wasn't really dead, but it made me ill at ease. Anne arrived with an ice-cold bottle of white wine, and Shelley came with a list. Then the doorbell rang; Anne answered it, returning with a dozen pink roses in her arms. The card read "I am thinking of you on this difficult day. Chuck." He was out of the country, but had arranged this before he left. How thoughtful. The tears flowed copiously from then on.

We sorted Carrie's clothes, her bass, and her albums. Everything. I was giving things away like some wild person. We found her diary, and we all agreed that it was filled with her secrets, not ours, so we destroyed it, unread. I kept some special things like her Grace Jones sweatshirt and her red flatties and the rings I had given her, but it was not enough. There would never be enough of her.

The following weekend, while visiting my sister's farm, I checked my phone messages at home on an old-fashioned answering machine, and there was one from Chuck. He had a nice voice. When I called him back, he asked to see me. He couldn't wait for our date the following week. I acquiesced, and we met the next day. This time, we went around the corner from my house for dinner and again had a pleasant time. He was wearing a big toothy goofy smile but, to my relief no aftershave. He was nothing like the men I was used to dating. Most of them were dark, sophisticated, smooth, and sexy, and drove fancy cars.

He asked if I wanted to meet his children, and explained again that they were the most important part of his life. I invited them to go swimming at my tennis club. In the pool, I held onto the youngest one, James, and he held tightly onto me. Big sigh. I loved the feel of that little body. The oldest one, Corby, pointed out the dog hair in the car, and mentioned that the dog belonged to Mary, Dad's girlfriend. Niels just watched me and said very little.

Chuck invited me for a fancy dinner at his yacht club on the island in the Toronto harbour. The food was only passable, like most clubs in those days, although the Dom Perignon was delectable. I had been wined and dined so much with that champagne that I didn't rave about it, as he expected.

I asked if I could call him Charles, because I hated the name Chuck. Aside from the fact that he was involved in a small family business, he didn't tell me much about his work. He did talk a great deal about his kids and about his estranged wife, who was a challenge.

I thought it appropriate to invite him for dinner. So we set a date for a weekend when he didn't have the boys and I could show off my cooking skills. There was no fire in my belly, but he was nice. He made me laugh, and was very upbeat and positive.

I decided to use the angel-hair pasta I had brought home from New York, and I bought a cooked lobster, extracted the meat, and served it with a light olive oil, lemon, and parsley sauce as a starter. I grilled a Rock

Cornish hen on my charcoal barbecue, split it, and served it with some sautéed carrots and French beans. For dessert, I had two small chocolate mousses with raspberries. As I was preparing the food, I wondered, *Why on earth am I going to so much trouble for this man? I am not even smitten.* Then, I rationalized that I loved cooking and, if we didn't continue dating, which was in the back of my mind, I wouldn't feel beholden for his dinners. Sure.

He talked nonstop about sailing and his other interests, but he also listened to me. He stared into my left eye, which drove me senseless. He explained that he was a photographer, and my eyes fascinated him, especially the one that was closest to him. I assumed he would make a move to take me upstairs to bed, but instead he just thanked me for the evening and kissed me goodnight.

A week later, I was eating popcorn and feeling depressed while watching on television the Wimbledon tennis semifinals with Boris Becker, whom I found rather boring. I was missing Carrie terribly, which was how I felt all the time. Tigger and I were cuddled on the couch. The phone rang, and it was Charles inviting me to a Christmas in July party at one of his friend's.

That party was a lift. Charles was good to be with because he paid attention to me rather than checking out all the other women in the room. So I invited him for Sunday dinner at my friend Kathleen's place. I had made the match between her and her husband, John, and knew I was always welcome in their home. After dinner, Charles asked if I would like to spend a weekend with him and his boys in Collingwood at his ski chalet. I turned him down. He seemed nice, but I really wasn't attracted to him enough to go to bed with him, which would be expected if we were away for the weekend.

Summer was moving along, and I had signed the CBC contract to start work in early September in Vancouver. I knew that I had to organize the unveiling of Carrie's stone before I left. There are rules about this—not sooner than a month after burial, nor longer than a year. I wasn't sure when I would return to Toronto.

I had no idea how torturous it would be to choose a stone, and foolishly didn't ask anyone to come with me. I was so independent that it never occurred to me. When I entered the monument store, I was devastated but managed to choose a pale pink heart-shaped stone. Along with the obligatory Hebrew for her name and dates, I included the line "She looks down upon the things of earth like some gentle star."

Arriving home I collapsed. This was not how it was meant to be in the natural order of things. No wonder the Jewish religion dictates that when you lose a parent, you officially mourn for a month; when you lose a spouse, you mourn for a year; but when you lose a child, you mourn forever. And it is true.

Charles didn't discourage easily. He again invited me away with his boys. I had already set the date for the unveiling, and it was the following weekend. I explained that I couldn't go because I would be preparing a small reception at my house. He replied, "I know you will have your ex-husbands there, but I would like to come, and give you moral support if only from a distance. I am a father after all."

I was amazed. "This is just like a funeral, with a cantor and prayers, and much grief." He responded, "I'll be there if you want." I was touched, and said yes. He then asked, "Why don't you come up to Collingwood for one night, and you can see the boys and perhaps that would cheer you?" The man never gave up.

I went to Collingwood with him and the three little boys. Dinner was at a pizza place and, even though they were young, they had mammoth appetites. I liked to pick the topping off the pizza and leave the crusts. They just gobbled them up. The kids were joyful and well behaved. Charles had brought pads of paper and markers for them, and they quietly drew pictures while we sat at the table in the restaurant.

At the chalet, they played for a while. Then Charles put them to bed without much fuss. I watched as he hugged them tightly, while they hugged back equally tightly, and then he tucked them into bed, saying goodnight.

I fell in love.

It was magic. He was such a good father, caring and firm, and the boys seemed delightful. I fell in love with all of them. I was wearing a very large T-shirt that night, with the words: THINK BIG. Charles and I went to bed together for the first time, and I was a goner.

All of a sudden, this man whom I hadn't found particularly attractive, became handsome. I loved his hair and his long legs and his love of music, even if it wasn't my kind. A blues and jazz fan, he introduced me to Alberta Hunter, Stevie Ray Vaughan, and Robert Johnson, among many others. He even arrived with a new invention called a CD player, and we listened to the tiny records that sounded so clear and took up a lot less space than my albums.

Aria- song of a life

He was happy, upbeat and positive, and he adored me. On the drive home, I just stared at his beautiful profile, with his turned-up nose, and admired his strong arms. Incredibly, I hadn't noticed any of this before. He dropped the boys off at their mother's house in the west end of Toronto in Etobicoke, and then we drove across the city to my place in Yorkville.

Later in my bedroom, he looked at me and said, "Would it scare you, if I told you that I love you?" It was touching to hear, but I was in such a vulnerable state, and the dog hairs were still in his car. I replied, "When you sort out your other relationship with your girlfriend, Mary, we'll see where this takes us. I'm not interested in sharing or in games. Just a simple committed relationship would suit me perfectly."

The unveiling of Carrie's stone was the following weekend. Mort arrived. He looked so small. It was a hot summer day, and the gravesite was filled with people. Anne and Ellen stood close by me, as did Robert and Mort. Robert was devastated. He had been such a good father to Carrie, but he wasn't a man to show his emotions. Neither was Mort.

The cantor started chanting; I started sobbing, and my girlfriends put their arms around me. Carrie's fathers kept their distance. My sister's family surrounded and held her, thank God, and Charles was somewhere quietly watching. Afterwards, we had food and drink at my place. Somehow I had organized it. Charles was completely at home. He was comfortable, and he was comforting to me. Mort had shaken his hand, but Robert wouldn't. He must have intuited the seriousness of our relationship. I believe that he thought he might yet return.

After everyone had gone, Charles stayed. He said he was in the process of letting Mary know that he was in love with me. He told me that he had never given her any indication that he was in love with her. He liked her, but it was over when he first saw me. Hearing him say that made me feel cherished. It was impossible to see myself through his eyes, and to imagine those eyes falling in love with me at first sight, but I tried.

I learned that Charles was the head of a family business in venture capital, Investors Finance. They had previously owned a company called Sterling Trust. It was a successful company, but Charles had taken it many steps further. My happy-go-lucky yuppie guy turned out to be an astute businessman. One of his ventures was in magazines, and he offered to have a staff designer organize a photo shoot for my album, which had been completed but was awaiting a cover and packaging. It wouldn't cost the record company or me anything.

The photographer was a top one, John Mastromonaco, who specialized in fashion. I spent hours with a makeup artist and posing for the shoot. Beforehand, I discussed the music of Kurt Weill, with its dark between-the-wars atmosphere. It was decided that black, white, and a slash of red would be the colour template.

I wore black net stockings and a lacy silk teddy, but all you could really see were my legs, my long hair, and an intense expression on my face. The makeup blanked out most of my features, but my cheekbones and eyes were visible and riveting. It was a captivating cover; so compelling that Charles convinced the printers to make giant posters of it. I still have hundreds in my basement, if anyone is interested. The photograph was extremely dramatic and received much attention. The record was reviewed everywhere, and my singing won praises. It even was featured in *People* and *Billboard* magazines. But, as flattering as it all was, I still ached for my Carrie.

One Sunday evening, Charles announced that he was going away with his boys for a week to Geneva Park, a family camping site near Orillia, Ontario. I was starting to get that hollow stomach feeling when he asked me to join them. Whew! He said that it would be a good time for me to meet his parents and sister's family, who had been vacationing there for years. It was pretty basic, but I would love it. He asked me to bring a trunk full of wine, as there was no liquor served in the dining hall, where we would be eating dinner at five o'clock each evening. It was simple fare, just a step above hospital food. *Bring on the jello and meatloaf.*

I was looking forward to this family vacation, and arrived on a sunny Monday morning. Charles helped me move in and suggested I put on a bathing suit and go to the beach with him and the boys. We were just starting our swim when he was summoned by phone to attend an urgent meeting in Toronto. He was in the middle of critical business negotiations and simply couldn't miss this meeting. I agreed to look after the boys.

I relaxed in an old Muskoka chair, with the kids around me playing on the beach. Jane, Charles's sister, introduced herself, along with her three daughters, all under the age of seven. Before I knew it, two-year-old Kate was on my lap, and the other girls were leaning in. Jane who had some errand, asked if I minded keeping an eye on the girls as well. I found it quite amusing and delightful being surrounded by young children. After about half an hour, a woman in her late sixties arrived; she bore a vague resemblance to Charles. "I can't believe that Chuck invited you here and just left you with all the kids. And where is Jane? I am Chuck's mother, Betty, by the way."

Later that evening in the dining hall, I met Mr. Petersen, Niels, and dozens of family friends. I liked Charles's family, who were warm down-to-earth people. As the week wore on, we swam, hiked, played on the swings, and sat singing lustily around campfires. I even took part in a Sunday church service and sang the "Lord's Prayer". The more I was with Charles, the more I fell in love. I started to wonder how I was going to sell my house and head off to Vancouver, feeling as I did about him, the boys, and his family.

After the Geneva Park experience, Charles said he wanted to get me something special to show his love, but he had noticed that I didn't have pierced ears. I quickly rectified that by going with Stephen to have my ears pierced. Stephen was my gay accompanist and confidante, the best kind of friend for a girl to have. If he hadn't been gay, I would have fallen for him, he was such a doll.

I told him I was in love but thought I should move to Vancouver anyway because I was in such a susceptible state. He agreed. He said, one day my heart would lead me in the right direction, but that I should leave to see if the relationship could hold. I put the move off until Labour Day, which would give me time to find an apartment before I had to start my job at the CBC. The earrings were perfect diamond studs.

The rest of the summer was tumultuous. After Charles told Mary that he was in love with me, she called one evening to tell him she was going to commit suicide. He went over to her place to save her, and I guess she changed her mind because she didn't do it. I was unimpressed because I knew that if she wanted to, she would have. I had no patience for that sort of ploy.

I needed to sell my house and get my furniture ready to be shipped to Vancouver. In a quick trip out West, I sublet a stunning penthouse condo overlooking Howe Sound, with two balconies, a romantic sky-lit bedroom, and a small den. It even had a fireplace and a bar, separating the kitchen from the living room. Although it was very small, it was filled with mirrors that made it seem larger. It was sparkling new and not far from where I had lived with Nanny Mac, eighteen years earlier. It was close to Carol Lang's apartment in Kitsilano, so I knew I wouldn't be lonely. Kits was a lively area—fish stores, bakeries, vitamin stores, vegetarian restaurants, Thai food, Chinese, trendy clothing stores, a classical record store, supermarket, everything—all walkable from my place.

I had borrowed a friend's sports car when I arrived to scope out the rentals, and drove around getting my Vancouver bearings. The only problem was that everywhere I kept seeing girls who looked like Carrie, with her long red hair, and I started following them, only to be disappointed. My emotions were mixed up. One part of me was wildly in love, and the other part as forlorn and sad as it was possible to be. I didn't stay long in Vancouver, as I wanted to rush back to be with Charles. Tigger was still in Toronto, waiting for me, too.

My singing career was on hold. After the recording, all my interest in performing faded, and I anticipated starting a new career as a television host out West. I packed up my house. Charles and I were in the midst of a chaotic time, dating and learning about each other. I knew that I had to leave to be sure that all the passion I felt for him and the boys was real. My sister and nephew were worried that I would be hurt. They were not so sure about Charles and warned me to be careful.

Charles and I spent our last weekend together at the Niagara-on-the-Lake winery of a mutual friend, Donald Ziraldo, or Z, as we affectionately called him. It was a festive time, with a superb dinner. Pierre Trudeau, who was no longer prime minister, was part of our group. It was good to see him again, although he wasn't happy with his chosen escort, who worked for the festival. He was accustomed to being paired with performers, actresses, and television personalities.

We all went to the opening of a brilliant Noel Coward play, *Cavalcade*, at the Shaw Festival. The evening was a glamorous black-tie event. Charles seemed to enjoy the limelight with me on his arm, experiencing my celebrity with all that implied. Two days later, I left Toronto by plane. My little black Renault Sport and many of my belongings, including Tigger, were already en route to British Columbia.

Soon after I reached my apartment, the phone rang—Charles welcoming me to my new home and wishing me well. He asked if he could come for a visit the following weekend, and naturally I said yes. The sky was blue, the air was clear, and I could see the mountains from my balcony. Vancouver had already started healing me once again, as it did after Whitehorse, except that Carrie was no longer a baby. Carrie was no longer.

I sighed and hugged her cat, then set about to get the place in order. Such a small space needed all the openness I could create. The sun streamed into my new home through the large windows. All the walls were newly painted off-white, and my sofa matched. No red anywhere. There were hardwood floors, and one wall of the bedroom space was mirrored, so I could see the view reflected when I lay in bed. There was a small balcony off to the side of the bedroom. It was very romantic, and I loved it. I hung my pictures and started nesting.

When I began work at the CBC's Broadcast Centre on Hamilton Street, everything was in order. Memories of my other sojourn in Vancouver flooded my mind as I crossed the Burrard Street Bridge and headed to work. Ron Devion, head of television there, made me feel at home. I had great respect for his imagination, energy, and organizational skills.

It didn't take long for me to get the feel of the place and my duties, which included producing items for the arts program I was hosting, *The Arts Today*. I did taped mini-interviews with performers and directors and the like to promote their upcoming shows. It was not complicated, and I learned quickly.

I was scheduled to appear on a comedy show *Downtown Saturday Night*, hosted by Pat Bullard, with some comedy sketches featuring people like Colin Mochrie, who was just starting his career. This show was not popular and was pulled very quickly. I was certainly not in my comfort zone. I did reports for Expo'86, which took me all over Vancouver to promote the arts in the festival. Along with being on camera, I had to produce my items. I learned about production, editing, and dealing with other artists as a producer/host. I quickly developed a work routine and looked forward to going to the CBC every day as well as getting regular paycheques.

I anticipated Charles's visits. I wasn't certain how it would play out, but when I picked him up at the airport each time, and we returned to my condo, I knew that I still loved him, and he was perhaps even more in love with me. We spent glorious weekends together, exploring places like Granville Island and Robson Street. We ate at The Cannery and other landmark restaurants, and it was hard to say goodbye on Sunday night. This was the beginning of our long-distance relationship. It was often hard to connect live by phone, with the time change. My old tape-recorder answering machine held promise, or frustration, for me when I arrived home from work.

Charles started coming every second weekend, which was when he didn't have the boys; he suggested that I fly to Toronto on the weekends when he did. Though we started that way, my salary just couldn't take it. I told him that if he wanted to see me, he would have to pay for my trips. After he agreed to this, we had some exhausting weekends. We were both in our early forties, and the lovemaking was nonstop, enhanced by the fact that four thousand miles separated us.

Then another traumatic event. My sister called to say she had been diagnosed with breast cancer and was due for surgery. I booked a ticket to Toronto. Carol and I were getting closer and closer, even though we were living farther apart. I realized during her hospital stay, just how much I loved her and needed her, and she me.

People didn't talk much about breast cancer in those days, and it didn't seem to be of the epidemic proportions that it is now, but maybe that was because no one talked about it. I was with her just before she went into surgery, and she had pinned a note on her breast to be sure there were no mistakes about which one it was. The nurse told me how well she looked, considering her age. The nurse had been reading the chart of an eighty-year-old woman instead of my forty-something sister. We shared a laugh over that one.

Carol had a lumpectomy, with radiation scheduled for her near future. Charles was with me during that emotional time; already, he was becoming part of the family. I had to return to Vancouver and my job, but I knew that my dear sister was on the mend.

Back in Vancouver, I was asked to take part in a fundraiser for the Anna Wyman Dance Theatre; and although I hadn't been performing, when I heard that the other performers would include Karen Kain, Veronica Tennant, Jeff Hyslop, and Toller Cranston, I agreed. It was held at the Queen Elizabeth Theatre, and I invited Charles to come. He would finally get a chance to hear me sing in front of an audience. He had the boys that weekend and decided to bring them out to Vancouver with him.

We did some touring around, but this was made difficult due to a freak November snowstorm and freezing weather. We went to see the famous St. Roch, a schooner owned by the RCMP that was the first ship to completely circumnavigate North America and the second to complete a voyage through the Northwest Passage. I continued to be

Aria- song of a life

fascinated by Charles's patient teaching of his sons about everything in minute detail. A sailor, he knew a great deal about the fine ships of the past. We walked through that magnificent schooner and learned much about naval history during our morning adventure. The boys came to my rehearsal at the theatre, so they could hear me sing and get the flavour of the performing arts without having to sit through the evening concert. I arranged for Carol Lang to stay with them, while we were out. One day, we took them to the television station where I worked, and they sat in the sound booth and watched me tape one of my shows. It was a memorable weekend for all of us.

My record had been released to much acclaim, and I was invited to give an intimate concert with piano at the Arts Club in Vancouver. Stephen, my accompanist and friend, came out and stayed at my apartment. We had not only a fine time artistically but a hilarious visit as well. Stephen had the most delightful wry sense of humour. I had promised to make him his favourite lamb kidneys in wine sauce as a reward, along with the fee he would receive.

We went out to lunch at Bridges, the Granville Island eatery, with some performer friends, and when the bill arrived, everyone put down cards so it could be split. Not only were there Visas and MasterCards as usual when folks divvy up a bill, but Sears, Salvation Army, hospital cards, you name it. We all sat straight-faced, when the poor waitress just stared at them perplexed.

One night, over a cognac, Stephen repeated what he had said earlier to me in Toronto when I asked him about Charles. "Just follow your heart. It will tell you what to do. Remember life is not a rehearsal."

When we had spent those few days in Geneva Park with his family, Charles asked me to spend Christmas with him and the boys. That was a really touching moment, because I hated the thought of being alone at Christmas. Even though I am Jewish, I am a cultural Jew at best. I like some of the traditions and the holidays, and saying, "Shabbat Shalom" to my sister, lighting candles on Friday nights when I remember, and when it suits me. But I love Christmas; and when that tradition started with the Whites and later with Robert and Carrie, I knew it would be the saddest time to be alone. Anyone who has experienced a loss of a loved one knows that it is the holidays, birthdays, and anniversaries, the milestones that ache the most. So when Charles said that we would be together, my heart soared.

Riki Turofsky

It was my turn to visit Toronto at the beginning of December. I bought a bright red dress, and looked my best. Charles took me out to the restaurant where we had met, the Westside Grill, and asked me to move back to Toronto to live with him. As pleased as I was at the prospect of sharing his home, I didn't want to be his children's father's girlfriend. I wanted status and most particularly I wanted family. I said that I would only come back if I were engaged to be married. Without skipping a beat he said, "Well I want a marriage contract."

I responded just as quickly, "That's fine with me. We will discuss it with our lawyers." Not very romantic, but agreed on. Charles had a difficult separation from his ex-wife. He had decided never to marry again. I guess I taught him never to say never. I will not go into details, but he was stung badly financially and ended up supporting her very generously. He was pleased to support his sons and did so way beyond what the Ontario laws demand.

A few weeks later, I was packed for the Christmas visit and heading back to Toronto. I still hadn't decided when I would leave Vancouver permanently. I invited all the Petersens for Christmas dinner at Charles's new home. He had actually purchased it one month before we met, and the main floor, except for the kitchen, was renovated. He had a designer choose beautiful furnishings, and most everything was creamy white. When she chose an ivory bedspread, I don't think she had taken little boys into consideration, nor a man who liked to drink coffee and eat pizza in bed, but it was design-magazine worthy.

I brought all my mother's sterling silver flatware with me, and bought a fresh turkey at a local butcher. I even had my magic cooking paper and set about to make a traditional Christmas meal. As it turned out, this was a good thing, because Charles' mother was a terrible cook. It was decided that his sister would do some meat pies or her version of tourtière for Christmas Eve.

A few days before Christmas, Charles and I went out to eat with my sister and Bernie in an Italian restaurant near their home. During dinner, Charles mentioned that he had a small Christmas gift for me and wondered if I would like it. He took Carol outside to show it to her and to get her approval. When they came back, she quietly told me to pretend I liked it so as not to hurt his feelings. When we returned to his house, I started to prepare for bed and saw a package on my pillow. Charles said he just couldn't wait to give me my gift until Christmas and hoped I would like it.

It turned out that my sister had been teasing me. I didn't have to pretend to like my gift. It was a magnificent gold Cartier Panthère watch. It fit perfectly on my wrist like a bracelet, and it was waterproof so I could wear it all the time. I had never coveted jewelry, basically because I couldn't afford it. After the losses I had experienced, material things just didn't mean much to me. But I had been reading *Town and Country* magazine, and I enjoyed looking at beautiful things. And there it was on my wrist, my own treasure.

Christmas dinner was enjoyable. The boys and the cousins arrived with huge appetites. Mr. and Mrs. Petersen brought overstuffed green garbage bags, filled with toys for all the grandchildren. In the front hall stood a very large freshly cut Christmas tree decorated by Charles's interior designer with petite china Victorian dolls on swings, among other fine objects.

Charles's mother found it difficult to believe that a Jewish girl could do a traditional Christmas dinner. In fact, I had been making turkey for years and using my magic cooking paper, so the bird was crisp on the outside and tender inside. In those days, I cheated on the stuffing, using Paxo, which had been Robert's recipe idea. I made an enormous quantity of peas and carrots and roast potatoes, and served pies for dessert.

After a few days in Toronto, I headed back to Vancouver and my life there. During Charles's visits, we spent the most romantic weekends, hiking through Stanley Park, eating in West coast restaurants, but mostly entwined in each other's arms. We hated saying goodbye. I decided to leave for Toronto permanently in the spring. Stephen had been right. My heart told me it was more important to live life, ro be part of a family, than to continue my television career in Vancouver.

I moved into Charles's house on Royal York Road, and unpacked most of my clothes. The movers were going to bring the furniture and my Kawai upright piano, although there was already a very fine baby grand piano in the living room. I would have to sort out where my piano would go, and thought it might be nice to gift it to Charles's sister for her three daughters to play. I tried to fit my clothes into the built-in closets and drawers in the bedroom dressing area. The design was sleekly attractive, but impractical—not nearly enough space for my things.

Charles and I climbed into the massive two-person whirlpool tub, where I started to cry. I had realized that I was living in someone else's house and had given up my freedom. It was starting to feel like a mistake until Charles laughed and told me to spread out and take as much room as I needed and to make his home my home. He consoled me because he knew I was also crying about Carrie. He started to cry with me and, before I knew it, I felt confident that I would be happy living with him.

The next afternoon, I was standing in the kitchen thinking that it really needed to be renovated, when the doorbell rang. I was handed a large box, filled with a dozen, deep red long-stemmed roses. I looked more carefully at them and saw one pink rose. And around its neck was a diamond engagement ring. The card simply read "Charles".

More tears. He remembered about my pink Carrie rose. The ring in the shape of infinity if you turned it on its side fit my ring finger perfectly. When he arrived home, we set a date. He still needed to get a divorce, even though he had been legally separated for almost three years, but we figured that a June wedding would allow us plenty of time. Charles managed the divorce and settlement with his ex-wife, although it wasn't easy. He gave her everything she wanted except himself. There would be joint custody, and I was up for that.

June 7 arrived very quickly. The wedding took place at my sister's farm in Caledon. It was officiated by a sympathetic Unitarian minister, Katharine Cook. The service was outside on the lawn leading down to a large pond where a wishing well stood. The weeping willows and all the greenery were a beautiful backdrop to the ceremony.

As we walked down the hill, my friends Diane Stapley and Pat Rose sang "Tonight I Celebrate My Love for You", accompanied by flute and guitar. My girlfriends, Anne and Ellen, along with two of Charles's best friends, held the *chuppah*, or canopy. My father-in-law read from the New Testament, and my brother-in-law read in Hebrew. I sang "One Hand One Heart" from *West Side Story*. Charles stomped on the wine glass. I said, "I love you with all my heart." He said, "I love you with all my soul."

It was really a '60s wedding in the '80s. The three boys looked adorable in white pants and blue blazers with pale blue shirts. My three nieces wore dresses in a blue spring flower pattern, although their father had forgotten them in Toronto and had to drive back to retrieve them. All the members of the wedding party wore blue. The florist was drunk and stoned and arrived late. The food was ahead of its time, chicken saté and lemongrass-stuffed barbecued salmon.

My sister arranged pink Billecart-Salmon champagne, with Riki and Charles written on the label. Her wine business was starting to flourish. An airplane flew overhead with a banner "Bravo Riki and Charles"; that was from Ev. After the service, it rained, and everyone ran for cover to the tent at the top of the hill by the house. And then, a rainbow appeared in the sky. Sniff....

We danced, and I sang with the Graham Howes jazz group I had hired for the dinner/reception. Fred Davis joined in, and played the trumpet. Everyone at that time knew him as a broadcaster and host of *Front Page Challenge*, but he was a terrific jazz trumpeter and pianist. Charles's best man gave an inappropriate speech about one of Charles's ex-girlfriends. I spoke, my sister spoke, and Charles spoke. There were about one hundred and fifty of us, including Mother and Father White, Neil and Sally, Mayor Art Eggleton, Charles's friends, my sister's family, my friends, and all three Carols.

A CITY television cameraman was hired to film everything in a very Robert Altman way. After the cake, our exhaustion, and exhilaration, we headed back to the city, climbed into our bed with the boys, and watched the wedding and the party on video. We had missed so much. The next day, before we headed off to France on a bicycle trip, we noticed a cardinal in our garden sitting on the fence, near our pink roses. Sniff again.

Riki Turofsky

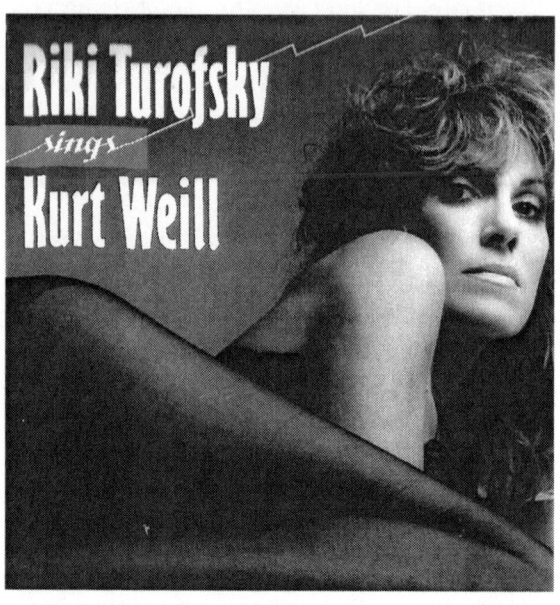

Riki Turofsky Sings Kurt Weill, photo credit John Mastromonaco, 1985

Riki and Sophia Loren before TV interview credit: candid snapshot taken by colleague 1986

Aria- song of a life

Charles and Riki, Niagara on the Lake, Trudeau in background, 1985

June 7, 1987, wedding at farm with Corby, James, Niels

Postlude —And Beyond June 2012–2014

I am sitting at the window in my airy office on the second floor landing of my home on Royal York Road. It's a beautiful evening, and the leaves of the old maple tree in front of me are swaying in the soft summer breeze. Photos surround me. My Queen Anne desk is covered with folders marked Projects, Travel, Arts, and Miscellaneous. There are Snoopy jokes on my corkboard and at least a dozen snapshots of me in golf foursomes at various tournaments. There's a luminous one of my sister at my wedding. Carrie's beautiful face is smiling in at least five pictures. There are the boys, as youngsters, at Geneva Park, where we spent many summers before we had our standard poodle, Sterling, now long gone. There's a small creased photo of my parents at the races, looking elegant in their hats and smart clothes, and one of me at age fifteen, sitting with Neil at his piano. I am singing.

There's another of me in Whitehorse General Hospital, holding a brand new baby girl. You can see the hospital identification bracelet on my wrist. On the wall is a photo of my daughter-in-law's, holding a one-year-old child, Rose, my granddaughter, with her pink cheeks and strawberry hair. And there is one with an older Rose in ballet gear posing with her two-year-old sister, June. I am surrounded by love and contentment.

I can hear the television blaring downstairs in our bedroom and know that Charles, a glass of red wine in his hand, is watching the nightly news. Little Bear, our rescue dog, is leaning against Charles and nudging him to have his tummy rubbed.

I will presently go downstairs and prepare dinner for just the two of us—Cornish hen, like that first important meal I cooked for him. As we do almost every night, we will have a bath together and discuss our day.

Aria- song of a life

I will have a glass of champagne, and he will continue with his red wine. Our marriage is stronger now than it was twenty-five-years ago, and we are still in the afterglow of an intimate anniversary celebration, just the two of us, at Langdon Hall.

Our marriage has had its rough spots, as most do, but we survived. It was not always easy being a stepmother, even though I was thrilled when the boys took up residence, and I nurtured and saw them through their teenage years. Their mother was perhaps my biggest challenge.

I played a lot of tennis, learned how to ski and sail, and laugh. I cooked more food than it is possible to imagine. Boys *can* eat. Mr. and Mrs. Petersen became Mom and Dad and spent many Sunday dinners at our home. I speak to Carol, my sister, every day, and we are best friends forever.

Now I am recovering from a knee replacement, already swimming, and healing well. Charles had throat cancer two years ago, even though he never smoked, but is now doing splendidly. We have booked a trip to France in a couple of weeks to relive our first trip together there many years ago. It all went by so fast. Charles says life is just a book with many chapters, and we keep moving on through them.

We are both retired, but busier than ever before, mostly with volunteer projects. Charles flies gliders and started a charity to enable people with disabilities to fly in gliders for inspirational flights and to learn to become pilots. I play golf, and have been a director on boards as varied as the Canada Council for the Arts and Food Banks Canada. I went back to the Opera School at the University of Toronto and headed up a very successful fundraising campaign to provide an endowment for future opera productions there. We both enjoy cycling together, particularly in places like Puglia and Provence. I sometimes sing for special occasions. But I don't miss performing. I love the young opera singers I hear now, and we are stalwart supporters of the Canadian Opera Company and the Stratford Festival.

We are eternally grateful to Princess Margaret Hospital for the fine treatment that Charles received there and support the hospital in a program that helps other patients on their journey through the healing process. I endowed a fund in Carrie's name at Mount Sinai Hospital. The money goes toward research for autoimmune diseases, with which we are surrounded. There is a plaque on the wall with her name on it.

I see her best friend, Shelley, from time to time, and am astounded that she has grown children, totally impossible for me to imagine Carrie with a child; if I do, I just want to weep. I am jealous of my girlfriends who have daughters who are alive and who spend time with them, very jealous. Big sigh.

I started this epilogue in 2012, and now it is the beginning of 2014. Takes time to write a book and get it published, it seems. As I review the book, I realize that I have forgotten to mention my sojourn in Rome, studying with Luigi Ricci, one of the great opera coaches, who worked with Puccini. He guided me through *La Traviata* in preparation for my many performances of the role of Violetta. I also forgot to mention Baby, Carrie's favorite doll that we carted around the country for years and finally had to take her for repairs to a doll hospital in Toronto. Forgotten too the wonderful CD that was made from lost tapes of my performances, discovered by a student, and has become my favourite recording. And the list goes on.

Our youngest son, James, is divorced, and we try to stay close to his children, our granddaughters, Rose and June, who are now seven and four. Although they live in Quebec, we go there as often as we can, and I Skype regularly. Our other two sons, Corby and Niels, live happily in Vancouver. We plan to go on a sailing trip with them and James next summer on the British Columbia coast. All my men are experienced sailors. I'll be in the galley.

Poor little Bear died of cancer in May, and we bought a schnoodle puppy named Oscar after my first opera role. Charles and I have become young and silly, playing with this little fellow, and it dawned on us, that he had better learn to play jazz piano, with a name like Oscar Petersen.

My sister's husband, Bernie, died over eleven years ago, and her long-time partner, Arthur, was hit by a car last winter in Toronto and died within a week. Carol and I are as close as ever, laughing, arguing, and sharing. We went to Israel and Petra in Jordan, just the two of us, for a brilliant hectic holiday this past October.

Charles and I entertain. We spend our winters in Florida, something we both said we would never do, and we love it. We travel a great deal, and just returned from a marvellous trip to the Galapagos. We take pleasure in our friends and our family.

I feel very blessed, despite this old wound of mine that won't heal. I never stop thinking about Carrie. I can't even imagine what she would be

Aria- song of a life

like at forty-eight. I still follow young redheaded women to see if there is a resemblance. I hate Mother's Day, even though I am a stepmother and a grandmother.

A friend of mine suggested that perhaps it was time to stop grieving. I wondered if that was possible, or should even be contemplated. And then recently, a lovely young woman gave me a card with a quote from Shakespeare's *Much Ado About Nothing,* and I understood at last: "Everyone can master a grief but he that has it."

Somehow though—when Charles reaches out to take my hand and holds me tight when I stand and stare forlornly at Carrie's grave and when I see the cardinals and pink roses in my garden and hear "I love you, Nana" from my little Rose and June in their sweet voices—I keep on track, and it is all worthwhile.

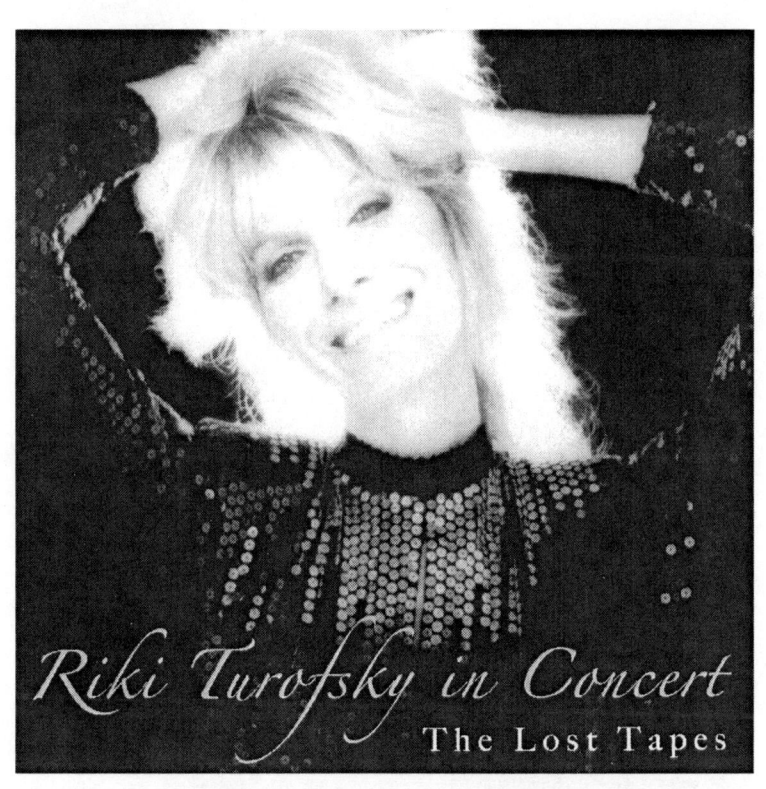

Riki Turofsky in Concert/ Lost Tapes, photo credit Cylla von Tiedemann 1985

Riki Turofsky

Riki A River so Long, photo credit Charles Petersen 1987

Niels Petersen Sr. (Dad's) 90th birthday

Aria- song of a life

Teenagers - James, Corby and Niels in Model
B Ford with Sterling and parents

Sisters in Israel 2014

Riki, June, James, Rose, Charles Christmas 2013

Charles, Riki and Oscar at home, photo credit Jennifer Wood 2014

Appendix—Career Highlights

1967
June: *Summer Serenade*, BC Opera Ensemble (first performance)
October: *Hansel and Gretel* (Gretel, Dew Fairy) Tour, BC Opera Ensemble, Vancouver Opera
December: Monteverdi *1610 Vespers*, Vancouver Bach Choir, Vancouver Symphony, Meredith Davies

1968
February: Haydn *Nelson Mass*, Vancouver Bach Choir, Beverley Fife
March: Mozart *Exultate Jubilate*, Renfrew United Church, Joyce Maguire
March: *Opera Night at the Symphony*, Vancouver Symphony, Meredith Davies
April: Menotti Double Bill, *The Telephone* (Lucy) and *The Medium* (Monica), BC Opera Ensemble
July: Puccini *La Boheme* (Musetta), Merola Opera of the San Francisco Opera, Stern Grove
August: Mozart *The Magic Flute* (Papagena), Merola Opera, Paul Masson vineyards
November: Rossini *Il Turco in Italia* (Fiorilla), Opera School, University of Toronto

1969
February: Humphrey Searle *Hamlet* (Ophelia), Opera School, U of T (world premiere)
March: R. Strauss *Ariadne auf Naxos* (Naiad), Opera School, U of T
November: Beethoven *Ninth Symphony* (soprano), Toronto Symphony, CTV television
September: Recipient, Canada Council Bursary

September: Scholarship Thank-you Concert for Canadian Opera Women's Committee
October: J. Strauss *Die Fledermaus* (Adele), Canadian Opera Company
December: Ravel *L'Enfant et les Sortilèges* (The Fire, The Princess), Opera School, U of T
December: Humperdinck *Hansel and Gretel* (Gretel), Hamilton Philharmonic, Boris Brott, televised
March: Mozart *The Impresario* (Mme. Hertz), Opera School, U of T

1970
May: Verdi *Un Ballo in Maschera* (Oscar), Vancouver Opera (official professional debut)
May: Montreal International Voice Competition (prize winner)
June: Graduation with Honours, Opera, U of T Faculty of Music
August: Nicolai *Merry Wives of Windsor* (Alice Ford), Music Academy of the West
September/October: *Don Giovanni* (Zerlina), Canadian Opera Company
September: Vaughan Williams *Riders to the Sea* (Nora), CBC Music Festival, Vancouver
October: Mendelssohn *Midsummer Night's Dream* incidental music (soprano), Hamilton Philharmonic, Boris Brott
November: Beethoven *Mount of Olives* (soprano), Hamilton Philharmonic (last-minute substitute)

1971
February: Stravinsky *Symphony of Psalms*, Hovaness *Magnificat* (soprano), Bach-Elgar Choir, Hamilton Philharmonic, Charles Wilson
April: Mahler *Symphony #2*, Edmonton Symphony Orchestra, Lawrence Leonard
April: Handel *Birthday Ode to Queen Anne*, Britten *Spring Symphony* (soprano), Festival Singers of Canada, Elmer Iseler
April/May: Offenbach *Tales of Hoffmann* (Olympia), Edmonton Opera, Vancouver Opera
May: Handel *Birthday Ode to Queen Anne*, Haydn *Nelson Mass* (soprano soloist), Festival Singers of Canada, St. John's Church, Smith Square, London; L'Eglise de la Madeleine, Paris
June: *Jenny Lind and Ole Bull* with Andrew Dawes, CBC Radio Festival

July: *Music at Midnight* Recital of Respighi, Stravinsky, Castelnuovo-Tedesco, Bernstein; pianist/conductor Raffi Armenian
August: Verdi *Rigoletto* (Gilda) with Louis Quilico, Ontario Place Toronto Symphony series
October: Bizet *Carmen* (Frasquita), Houston Grand Opera
October: Verdi *Un Ballo in Maschera* (Oscar), Edmonton Opera
November: Offenbach *Tales of Hoffmann* in concert (Olympia, Giudetta, Antonia), Kitchener-Waterloo Symphony
December: Britten *Les Illuminations*, McGill Chamber Orchestra, Alexander Brott

1972
September/October: Puccini *La Boheme* (Musetta), Canadian Opera Company
October: Mozart *Così Fan Tutte* (Fiordiligi), Chatanooga Opera
October: Bizet *Carmen* (Frasquita), New York City Opera
November: Handel *Solomon*, Toronto Mendelssohn Choir and National Arts Centre Orchestra, Elmer Iseler
December: Handel *Israel in Egypt*, Kingston Choral Society and Kingston Orchestra

1973
January: Donizetti *Daughter of the Regiment* (Marie), Houston Grand Opera
March: Glière *Concerto for Soprano*, Opera Arias, Victoria Symphony tour, Laszlo Gati
April: Britten *Les Illuminations*, CBC Vancouver Chamber Orchestra, John Avison
May: Variety Concert, Opening Ontario Place Summer Season
June: Handel *Messiah*, Toronto Mendelssohn Choir, Ontario Place, Elmer Iseler (6,000 in audience)
June: Verdi *Rigoletto* (Gilda), Canadian Opera Company, Ontario Place
July: Strauss *The Great Waltz* (Hélène Vernet), Milwaukee Operetta Festival
August: Glière *Concerto for Soprano*, Toronto Symphony, Ontario Place, Walter Susskind
September: Wolf-Ferrari *The Secret of Suzanne*, CBC Festival of Music, Vancouver
October: Concert of Opera Arias, Windsor Symphony, Matti Holli

November: *An Evening with Jenny Lind*, Sarnia Concert Association, Stuart Hamilton accompanist
December: Haydn *The Creation*, Kitchener-Waterloo Symphony, Raffi Armenian

1974
January: Honegger *King David*, Toronto Symphony Orchestra, Elmer Iseler
February: Du Maurier Family Pops, Glière *Concerto*, London Symphony, Clifford Evens
March: Duet Recital with Judith Forst, St. Lawrence Centre for the Arts
April : Beethoven *Symphony No. 9*, Winnipeg Symphony, Piero Gamba
April: Orff *Carmina Burana*, Atlantic Symphony, Klaro Mizerit
April: Orff *Carmina Burana*, Hamilton Philharmonic, Boris Brott
May: Orff *Carmina Burana*, Vancouver Symphony, Kazuyoshi Akiyama
May: Haydn *Nelson Mass*, National Arts Centre Orchestra, Brian Law
Aug: Viennese Concert, Toronto Symphony, Franz Allers
October: Thomas *Hamlet* (Ophelie), Opera in Concert (inaugural)
November: Viennese Concert, Hamilton Philharmonic, Boris Brott
December: Gala New Year's Viennese Concert, Vancouver Symphony, Kazuyoshi Akiyama

1975
January/February: Verdi *Rigoletto* (Gilda), Vancouver Opera
February: Mozart *Requiem*, Thunder Bay, Dwight Bennett
February/March: Tibor Polgar and George Jonas *The Glove* (Princess), Prologue to the Performing Arts School tour with Andrea Martin and Martin Short
April: Concert with Harpist Erica Goodman, National Arts Centre
May: Orff *Carmina Burana*, Toronto Symphony, Elmer Iseler
June: Handel *Messiah*, Mendelssohn Choir, Toronto Symphony, Ontario Place, Elmer Iseler
June: Gay Nineties Concert, Hamilton Philharmonic, Ontario Place, Boris Brott
July: Viennese Concert, Toronto Symphony, Ontario Place, Victor Feldbrill
September/October: Mozart *Marriage of Figaro* (Susanna), Puccini *La Boheme* (Musetta), Kansas City Lyric Opera
October: Viennese Concert, Thunder Bay Symphony, Dwight Bennett
November: *The Glove* (Princess), Televised for CBC

December: Orff *Carmina Burana*, Edmonton Symphony, Pierre Hétu

1976
June: *Of Mice and Men* (Curley's Wife), Netherlands Opera
June: Villa-Lobos *Bachianas Brasileiras*, Hamilton Philharmonic, Ontario Place, Boris Brott
July: Olympic Concert with Louis Quilico, Montreal Symphony, Boris Brott
August: Kalman Countess Maritza (title role), Toronto Symphony, Ontario Place, Franz Allers
September: Duet Recital with Judith Forst, Queen Elizabeth Playhouse, Vancouver
October: Glière *Concerto*, Windsor Symphony, Matti Holli

1977
January: Cabaret Concert Viennese, London Symphony, Brian Jackson
January: Family Pops, Toronto Symphony, Erich Kunzel
May: Mozart *The Marriage of Figaro* (Susanna), Thunder Bay
Summer: *Evening in Vienna*, Hamilton Philharmonic, Ontario Place, Boris Brott
September: Lehar *The Merry Widow* (title role), Hamilton Philharmonic, Boris Brott
October: Oktoberfest Vienna Concert, Kitchener-Waterloo Symphony, Raffi Armenian
November: Verdi *La Traviata* (Violetta), Canadian Opera Company, Halifax
Fall-Winter: Du Maurier Search for Stars Judge, continuing series across Canada (7 years)
December: Viennese Night, Vancouver Symphony, Erich Kunzel

1978
January: Schafer *Hymn to Night*, CJRT Orchestra, Paul Robinson (composed for Riki)
January: Singing for Queen Elizabeth, Toronto
January: *Evening in Vienna*, National Arts Centre Orchestra, Erich Kunzel
March: *An Evening with Jenny Lind*, CBC Newfoundland, Stuart Hamilton accompanist
April: Verdi *La Traviata* (Violetta), Mozart *The Marriage of Figaro* (Countess), Canadian Opera Company
June: Britten *A Midsummer's Night Dream* (Titania), National Arts Centre

November: Floyd *Of Mice and Men* (Curly's Wife), Netherlands Opera

1979
January: Britten *Les Illuminations*, Chamber Players of Toronto, Marta Hidy
April: Viennese Concert, Windsor Symphony, Matti Holli
April: Schafer *Hymn to Night*, Thunder Bay Symphony, Dwight Bennett
August: Schafer *Hymn to Night*, Peninsula Music Festival, Michael Charry
October: Viennese Concert, International Symphony Sarnia, Brian Jackson
November: Schafer *Hymn to Night*, National Arts Centre Orchestra, Mario Bernardi
December: Family Christmas Concert, Toronto Symphony, Victor Feldbrill

1980
Summer: Host, Summer Festival, CBC Television series
August: *Evening in Vienna*, Kingston Symphony, Alexander Brott
December: *Evening of Kurt Weill*, Toronto Arts Productions, St. Lawrence Centre

1981
January: Viennese Concert, Quebec Symphony Orchestra, James de Priest
June: Special Gala Viennese Concert, Kitchener-Waterloo Symphony, Raffi Armenian
October: Weill *Seven Deadly Sins*, Hamilton Philharmonic, Boris Brott
October: *Evening on the Danube*, Etobicoke Symphony, Eugene Kash
November: Tribute to *Hockey Night in Canada*, Windsor
December: Wolf-Ferrari, *Il Segreto di Susanna*, Netherlands Promenade Orchestra, Leo Dreihuys; Schafer *Hymn to Night*, Radio Philharmonisch, Lukas Vis

1982
April: Glière *Concerto*, Victoria Symphony, Paul Freeman
April: Royal Constitutional Gala (Host), National Arts Centre, in presence of Queen
April: Viennese Concert, Kitchener-Waterloo Symphony, Brian Jackson
Summer: *Celebrity Tennis*, CBC Television (series)
July: *Together* Concert with Kathryn Moses and Sylvia Tyson, Harbourfront
September: Schafer *Hymn to Night*, New Music Concerts, Walter Hall

September: *An Evening on Broadway*, Victoria Symphony, CBC Television, Paul Freeman (Actra nominee)
October: Pops Concert, Orchestra London, Alexis Hauser
November: *Today's Special is Opera*, TVO featured opera singer, Children's series

1983
February: Pergolesi *La Serva Padrona*, New Chamber Orchestra, Toronto
March: Weill *The Seven Deadly Sins*, Stratford Summer Music, Richard Ouzounian director
October: *Ein Berliner Cabaret*, Hart House
November: *An Evening in Canada*, Canadian Embassy, Washington, Stephen Woodjetts accompanist
November: *A Night in Vienna*, Okanagan Symphony, Leonard Camplin
December: New Year's Viennese Night, Delaware Symphony, Gerhard Track

1984
January: Cole Porter Celebration, Thunder Bay Symphony, Dwight Bennett
April: Mendelssohn *Elijah*, Vancouver Bach Choir, Vancouver Symphony, Kazuyoshi Akiyama
May: *The Curtain Rises* Concert, Northern Arts Centre, Yellowknife
August: *Some Enchanted Evening*, Victoria Symphony, Laszlo Gatti
November: Berlin Cabaret, Belleville
November: Britten *Les Illuminations*, Ensemble Ernest MacMillan, Hamilton, Marta Hidy

1985
March: Pops Concert, Pueblo Symphony, Gerhard Track
April: Carrie dies
June: *Riki Turofsky Sings Kurt Weill*, recording

Post-1985
A smattering of fundraisers, a private concert or two, and then the voice quietens in sadness

1987–2014

Arbor Award for volunteerism; Queen's Jubilee medal awarded twice for making a difference to Canadian life; plaques in Princess Margaret, St. Michael's, and Mount Sinai Hospitals for benevolence; honours at Stratford and Canadian Opera Company as a major donor; board member of the Canada Council for the Arts (full term of 6 years); board member of Food Banks Canada (full term of 6 years); president of University Faculty of Music Alumni Association and leader of campaign for endowment to Opera School Production fund.

Recordings
1978: R. Murray Schafer's *Hymn to Night*, shared album with Maureen Forrester
1980: *Jade Eyes*, a guitar/voice duet recital with Michael Laucke
Post-1987: *A River So Long*, recording for Charles of easy listening material, Lou Pomonti
2006: *Riki Turofsky in Concert: The Lost Tapes*, taped performances with orchestras, recorded at various concerts by CBC radio, created as a CD by Riki, and her favourite because it showcases her voice at its very best in live performances

About the Author

Riki Turofsky has sung with every major symphony orchestra and opera company in Canada, and many in the USA and Europe. She has been a television broadcaster, has five recordings, received the Arbor Award for volunteerism, and Queen's Jubilee Medal for her contribution to Canadian life. This is her first book.